Start Me Up

A Practical Guide

To Understanding Your Vehicle

Mike Davidson

"The Auto Guy"

www.MikeTheAutoGuy.com

Start Me Up

A Practical Guide

To Understanding Your Vehicle

What You'll Learn By Reading This Book:

- ➢ Car Care Basics

- ➢ Tips on Buying A Vehicle

- ➢ The Truth About Extended Warranties

- ➢ A "How To" Section

- ➢ How "The Auto Guy" Got Started

Start Me Up

A Practical Guide

To Understanding Your Vehicle

First Printing: July 2013

ISBN # 978-0-9883878-4-3

The Auto Guy

Parkway Automotive

708 Kirk Road

Little Rock, AR 72223

(501) 821-6111

Endorsements

"Congratulations, Mike, on writing a book that needed to be written—but more importantly, that needs to be read. This is a tough subject for the majority of vehicle owners, but the fact is you can't ignore your daily ride (your vehicle). Current vehicles are packed with computers, electronics and warning lights that often make funny noises, flash important messages and may slow your vehicle down or prevent you from starting your engine.

Current technology has made servicing your own vehicle far too complex for the average guy, but not for the "Auto Guy". I have known Mike, the "Auto Guy", for years and his history and passion revolve around customer service. I am the owner of TLC Daily Rental, and I have owned in excess of a thousand vehicles in the last twenty (20) years. Times have changed, vehicles have changed and maintenance schedules have changed; but Mike has kept pace with industry standards, which include technician training and the need for improved customer service.

While reading Mike's book I became aware of vehicle service requirements and information about the dashboard warning system that I did not previously know. Every owner should become familiar with Mike's list of acronyms and be alert to the dashboard warning lights.

Taking "ownership" of your vehicle is a must (and means more than simply having your name on the title) and calling the "Auto Guy" can provide your ride with the care it deserves. Proper scheduled maintenance will normally keep the warning light off. Be responsible-- read this book!"

Brent Tyrrell
Owner TLC Daily Rental
Little Rock Arkansas

"Mike Davidson; The Auto Guy, is a great coach for those who are intrigued about vehicle repair and maintenance. His insightful layman's review of vehicle components and upkeep can help every vehicle owner feel more empowered to converse with their transportation professional. This is a mandatory read before you face the next conversation with your mechanic."

Jim Murphy
Automotive Industry Coach

"Over the years I have read hundreds if not thousands of books, and I must say, this is one that is a must-read. Not only is it a great insight as to how a world-class auto repair shop owner thinks and lives his life, but the information Mike provides should be taught in every school in America. Learning how to drive is one thing, but learning how to find the right mechanics, and how to take good care of a vehicle, is something that we all need to know. Fortunately, Mike has now provided us with a guide that every motorist should read, but it's a book that should be passed on to our family and friends. There is no question, once you start reading this book two things will occur. You'll find it hard to stop, and when you do finish it, you will thrilled with what you have discovered."

Bob Cooper
President, Elite Worldwide, Inc.

"Mike Davidson has found yet another way to serve others. Through these pages he shares practical wisdom from his 20+ years in this industry. You'll enjoy learning about his background, why he operates his business as he does, and how to properly care for your vehicle. Mike has built Parkway to be one the Top 2% of independent repair shops in the country, coaches other shops across the nation and excels at giving the finest service imaginable to his customers. This is a great resource for everyone who drives a vehicle. It's Funny, Informative and Factual. Read this book! You'll be glad you did."

Michael DeLon
Parkway Automotive Customer

"Mike Davidson has written a simple, easy-to-understand guide to better understanding your car and how to take care of it. It's a good read for the beginning driver and also for those of us who haven't kept up with the changes in automotive technology over the years. Mike explains common acronyms, gives tips on maintenance and helps with bigger picture dilemmas like how to buy a used car. His section on when to buy a newer vehicle was particularly valuable for me. It's a worthwhile read and you're sure to be better friends with your car when you finish the book."

Larry Mougeot
Parkway Automotive Customer

"This book is based on the foundation of Christian beliefs held by Mike Davidson, his family and his staff. He understands and expects each of them to exhibit true personal care to each customer. That is rare in most businesses today. It is a value system that is delivered by how his staff treats customers, delivers integrity in service and fair charges. This easy-to-read book gives you inside secrets and helpful tips for any of us non-mechanical people!"

Tim Orellano, PHR
President - The Human Resources Team

Table of Contents

Foreword

My relationship with Mike "The Auto Guy" started as the result of an accident on black ice one morning on my way to work. I had only been in Arkansas for a month, but there I was in the dark on I-530 against the cement barrier facing traffic.

I can only surmise that the guy driving the wrecker knew of a shop off I-30 that helped out a lot of people. And so I went. The first experience with Mike was one of "service". He actually "wanted" to help and perhaps he knew how important it was for a customer to feel that repairs/service would be done honestly for a fair price.

As the years passed, the Pinto was traded for a vehicle with air conditioning (this Colorado girl didn't know that air conditioning was standard equipment in some parts of the country) and I continued to return to the shop where Mike worked.

When Mike decided to venture out with his own shop the decision was a no brainer—I would stick with the "one" I knew. The years passed and the Pinto turned into a Prelude. Then the Prelude (over 250,000 miles and still running strong) was traded for a bigger vehicle, a 1995 Chevy Silverado and the story continues. WE now are at 475,119 miles on the original engine & transmission! Yes, I said 475k!!

But with all the repairs and service one event that happened still has me shaking my head and saying "Wow!"

was the time Mike personally left a message on my answering machine telling me that I was "overcharged" $20 on a visit, and asking if I would like a check mailed or a credit on my next repair. "What?!?" It was only twenty dollars!! Whether a clerical error or one on the cost of a part, who calls to admit such a thing? I would have never noticed nor missed the money, but the standard practice at his shop is that they review receipts to make sure all is well. He felt the money, no matter how much or little, wasn't his and he was determined to settle the books.

So bottom line, Mike is genuinely concerned about people and helping. He's honest in business and quick with a smile and a laugh. Care for my vehicles through the years has really been a great collaboration. I know Parkway Automotive staff "have my back."

"The Auto Guy" with Shirley Scott

Shirley Scott
Parkway Automotive Customer
July 2013

Why I wrote this book

The car was originally designed to replace the horse. In fact it was originally called the "horseless carriage". Its sole purpose was to help us get places faster, and to make our work easier. There was a time in history where everyone knew about cars. And most knew how to care for them. Each car seemed to take on the owner's personality. You could see a car coming toward you and you would know exactly the kind of car it was. Today it's different. Currently there are approximately 44 different nameplates with 211 different models to choose from with endless number of sub models. The car is now a means to an end. It literally touches all walks of life.

With the speed of our culture and the advancement of technology being so fast, knowing about your car is nearly impossible unless you live and breathe it as I do. I constantly meet people who describe how they used to look under the hood and know the name of every part they could see. Today those same people will not even raise the hood, as they are too scared to look. I have met mothers, fathers, single moms and dads who wished they knew more about their car so that they could be sure that their children or loved ones would feel more comfortable with car ownership. That's why I wrote this book.

My heart's desire is first to serve people. To help them in any way I can. There is a biblical instruction that teaches me that if someone in need crosses my path, and if I have the resources to meet their need, I don't just say, "go be warm and be fed". Instead I am to serve, to help, to meet the need. I see a need for people to know not only how to take care of the car they currently have but to gain wisdom when it comes to replacing it with a new or used one. So here it is—the self-help book of car ownership. It won't make you a Master Certified Auto mechanic, but it will help you know what to do to keep you, your family, and your car safe.

Safety is a primary objective every time you get in a car. We pray for travel mercies. We tell our children to drive safely. Road signs tell us to drive safely, to wear our seat belts, and obey traffic laws, all so that we will "arrive alive" at our destination. Cars were never meant to be phone booths, texting stations or music halls. They were meant to help us arrive safely. Most of the technology advancements have an underlying theme of safety, many of which are addressed in these pages. More importantly, in these pages you will find simple helpful information on car ownership. Armed with the knowledge of car ownership, understanding what all the warning signs are, and knowing what to do when things go wrong will help all of us stay safe in and around our automobiles. So consider me the dad you never had who desires for you to know how to care for your car and arrive safely. If you have a specific question that I can answer, simply go to www.miketheautoguy.com

Mike Davidson, AAM, ASE
ASE Master Automotive Technician
July 2013

Acknowledgements

It is to my beloved wife, Nancy, of over 20 years that I give my heartfelt thanks for the loving care and support she has given, allowing me to spend the time necessary for training and learning about the automobile business. She has cared for our home, raised our children well, and freed me to be able to excel in my industry.

Each of our four children, Jenni, Jeff, Jerry, and John, have been instrumental in helping me to be a better father, husband, and business owner. Just knowing that my children are watching is reason enough to cause me to pay more attention to how I run my business

I want to acknowledge Michael DeLon for having the desire to go into marketing and help small business people like me fully understand how the focus of any type of marketing should always be on our customers. Without Michael and the team at Paperback Expert, you would not be reading this book.

I also want to express my appreciation to Bob Steel who came up with the title for this book.

Jim Murphy has been a large part of my training. I have been associated with Jim since the fall of 1999, and he continues to put in front of me the training needed to excel in my industry. He has played a huge role in challenging me to become better at whatever I do.

The editors B.G. Viner of Beyond Graphics and Larry Mougeot, customer and friend, spent countless hours making this book grammatically correct and fun to read. They are two of my life's cheerleaders.

My deepest, most heartfelt acknowledgement is to my Lord and Savior Jesus Christ. It is He who has made me who I am and continues to mold me into His likeness. In all that I do, I pray that I may do it for His glory, and not my own.

An Unexpected Gift

My youngest son had just purchased his dream car, a 1976 Corvette. Before he even drove it down the street, he made the decision that it would make a perfect get-away car for his sister and her new husband on their wedding day.

Within three days of owning his "Vette," John and I had cleaned it up nicely and surprised the happy couple with a gift no one would have imagined possible. You should have seen the look on their faces as they drove away in that great American sports car!

That's how John helped his sister get her start in marriage. I'll tell you more about John

and his Corvette later in the book, but now let me tell you how I got my start as "The Auto Guy."

The Birth of "The Auto Guy"

The year was 1969 and I was about five years old. I really loved my mom and I wanted to help her out. I distinctly remember sitting in the car one day and watching a man take a hose and put it in a hole in the side of the car. As I watched him I thought, "I can do that. I can help Mom with that!"

A few days later while her car was parked in our driveway, I glanced around and wouldn't you know—there was a hose! I picked it up, put it in the hole in the side of mom's car, just like the man at the service station had done. Well, as it turned out, it was gasoline he was putting in her car, not water! My heart was there. I really wanted to help, but I had filled her tank all the way up with water. Fortunately, I lived to tell about it, and the car was okay too.

I've gained some experience since then, and today I'm an ASE Master Technician. (ASE stands for Automotive Service Excellence and is our industry's credentialing organization.) You should make certain that anyone who works on your vehicle is ASE certified. It will give you confidence knowing that they have received the proper training to service your vehicle and have the education necessary to work on today's vehicles.

With the technology behind today's vehicles, my staff and I consistently attend classes and training events that enable us to stay on the cutting edge. Keeping ourselves sharp allows us to service our customers with excellence.

The Early Years

Learning how to treat customers began by watching my mom's work ethic as I was growing up. She was a single mother of three children and my earliest memories are those of her being an extremely hard worker. I not only learned to work hard, but more importantly I realized that learning and education never stop.

Mike's mom is featured in the company brochure.

When I was a fifth grader, I remember coming home from school at three o'clock and Mom arriving home shortly after five from her day job. After we had dinner together, she would take a nap. She always woke up in time to tuck me into bed, go to her night job at eleven o'clock, and work until morning.

I remember her working as a waitress at Denny's Restaurant. She learned that treating her customers well was of utmost importance. When I think about customer service, what my mom taught me was not just hard work, but to really *own* the needs of each customer. The word *empathy* also needs to be in your vocabulary and in your actions. When we have empathy in our mind and in our actions, we can put ourselves in the customer's shoes and ask ourselves, "What is their greatest need?" Only then are we able to consider what resources we have to meet that need and begin pulling them out.

As we grow in our business, we must continue to grow in our resources so that we can continue to meet the personal needs of every customer each time he or she comes in. They are going to have different needs. Their state of mind is going to be different. What they've experienced in the last week is going to be different. I need to make sure that I take time to see where their needs are on that day and look for ways to meet those needs, whether they relate to my business or not.

Let's say we receive a call from a customer whose car has broken down on the side of the road. They need two things. They need their car taken care of – that's why they called in the first place — but they have other needs,

since they hadn't planned on this happening. There is undoubtedly someplace they were going besides the side of the road. The first thing

The Parkway Courtesy Shuttle with driver, Jim Viner

we'll handle is getting the tow truck expedited. Next, and more importantly, we will help them get to where they were going. The best way to do that is to send someone after them and take them wherever they need to go. (*We have a FREE customer shuttle to do this very thing.*)

Here is another example of meeting the customer's needs. When a customer has left their vehicle with us to be serviced or repaired while they are out of town and are returning over the weekend, wouldn't it be nice if they found their car waiting for them in their driveway, ready to go, rather than at Parkway Automotive?

We work diligently to know our customers and understand their needs so that we can provide them with amazing customer service. We've found that when we do this, our customers not only appreciate our efforts, their level of trust in us goes up significantly and they refer their friends and family to us. That's how our business has continued to grow for many years. And it all started with my mom.

The Auto Guy's First Job

I began my career working for a GMC Truck dealership. My job was to be on the Detail Team. In fact, I *was* the team! I distinctly remember that the wash bay was outside, and my job was to make every new vehicle look presentable to the customer. To make sure I did it correctly, the owner, Brent Tyrrell, came out to the wash bay himself to show me how he wanted this done.

It was a cold November day in Arkansas and we were standing outside when Mr. Tyrrell said, "I want you to stand right here." I stood where he told me and watched as he washed a truck. When he finished, he came over to me, pointed to the newly washed truck, and said, "Mike, that's what I want my trucks to look like when you get done with them. Do you have any questions?"

"No sir," I said emphatically!

That was 1983, and I learned a very important principle from that experience.

Make sure the people who work for you know what you expect of them.

That was a profound learning experience for me, and I've retained it throughout my career. When my employees are not doing what I expect of them, instead of getting frustrated, my first thought is, "I probably haven't 'washed the truck' for them." I'll go back and 'wash the truck'. Then we'll sit down and talk about what I expect from them and look for ways to move forward. This process resolves a lot more issues than letting everything pile up, becoming frustrated, then having a discussion that's not so cordial. It follows the axiom:

Inspect what you expect.

While exceeding my customers' expectations and providing *"Service That Will Amaze You"* as our slogan says, I've learned that I need to "wash the truck" for each and every position and employee. When I do this, my employees can fully understand WHAT to do and WHY it needs to be done that way. Consistency is important in satisfying our customers, and the best way to be consistent is to make sure you are communicating clearly. "Washing the truck" is a phrase I use that reminds me to communicate clearly to my team so we can provide consistently excellent customer service every day.

More Than Repairing Cars

There's a word that many people don't like, but is a part of every business. That word is "sales." Sales are a part of every job of every business for anybody that does anything. I can't think of a single industry where everyone involved is not part of sales at some level. But when communicating with the customer one on one, be it eyeball to eyeball or on the phone, the job of the sales person is really a transfer of beliefs or ideas from one person to another. Selling is not trying to make a person buy something they don't want; it's a transfer of beliefs. It involves trust.

By having the technical background that I possess, I'm able to communicate to the customer not just that they need a certain "widget" (meaning any component or service), but why they need a widget, and how it will benefit them to have the widget. For me, I must believe in that widget, own that widget, and use that widget for my own vehicles, not just have the knowledge to talk about it.

For example, I would not want to talk with a consumer about having their transmission flushed every sixty thousand miles if I were not doing that on my own vehicle, my wife's vehicle, and my children's vehicles. That's a belief system I have because I know the transmission will last longer by having the fluid changed on a regular basis. That's my belief system, so I'm able to communicate with my customer with empathy because I know *why* their transmission ought to be flushed and how it will benefit them.

It's really a matter of trust and integrity with me. I'm not going to recommend that you do something that I'm not doing myself. **Trust occurs when people are so convinced you will do everything in your power for their good and nothing for their harm.**

Owning the Call

If there's one thing that drives me crazy, or at least gives me great concern, it's when I call a business and the person answers the phone and says, "Thank you for calling. To whom may I direct your call?" This communicates to me that they either can't or don't want to help me. It's as if somehow I'm supposed to know where it is I want them to send me and who it is at their company (whom I don't yet know) that is supposed to be able to answer my question or solve my problem. That's an all-too-often scenario that I encounter.

www.MikeTheAutoGuy.com

Another scenario is when I call a business, someone answers the phone, and I say the name of a person who works there. They reply, "Hold on please." I hear a click and they put me on hold. I may have been able to get the information I needed from the person answering the phone, but I thought I was talking to John when it was really Joe that picked up the phone. I say, "John" and he says, "No," and presses the hold button, never asking if there is something he can answer for me or help me with.

So in both scenarios I just described, if we "own" the phone call, what we would say to the customer is, "Thank you for calling Parkway Automotive. This is Mike. How may I help you?" Then there should be a pause to listen and understand what the caller's need is (*back to meeting the needs of our customer*). Many times you can assist the caller if you sincerely listen to their need. Often you can do this without having to be transferred to another person. Sometimes it can be as simple as taking a message. When a message is taken from a customer, you should then say to that customer, "My name is Mike. I will be sure John gets your message."

THAT is what I call "owning" the call. And it adds great value to the person on the other end of the phone because you are treating them with respect and doing everything you can to meet their need.

How many times have you called a business, only to hang up lacking confidence that the person taking your information is going to deliver your message to the person who needs it? At Parkway Automotive, before we end the phone call, we tell the customer who we are and that we're going to make sure that the person they were calling for gets the message.

Sometimes it is necessary to put the customer on hold. When that must happen, we should ask for permission to put you on hold *and* reassure you that if the person you're asking for isn't able to get to the phone in a reasonable amount of time, we'll pick up the line again. We won't just leave you on the phone in an eternal hold mode.

Most phone systems have some type of an alarm when someone's been on hold for a long period of time. That is still your phone call and until the other person picks it up, YOU "own" it. So you should do everything you can to own that call and try to meet the needs of that customer who is on the phone every time without a transfer. That is "owning" the phone call. It is your phone call until it has been given to another person. It's your responsibility. That's how you "own" the phone call.

At the end of the day, that caller really is your customer because they are all customers of your business. That's what I mean when I say that everybody is in sales. Without sales, there would be no business, and a big part of sales is meeting the customer's needs and treating them with respect.

In our business, and I believe in every business, the single thing that every consumer looks for is *trust.* Everything you can do to communicate trust will benefit your company. So we tell the customer that we care about them by:

asking permission to put them on hold,

assuring them I will deliver their message,

or

returning to the phone call after putting them on hold for a reasonable amount of time.

All three of these things, including taking the car back to their home when they're out of town or going to pick them up on the side of the road when their car is broken down, illustrate that *we care*. When you communicate that you care, you have also communicated that *you can trust me!* And that's how we have tried to build our business at Parkway Automotive.

Why Parkway?

With so many options available to you for vehicle repair, why should you choose Parkway Automotive? Let me begin by saying that the one reason you would want to do business with Parkway Automotive is the people who work here. That's Number One.

You're going to find people you can trust. You're going to find people who know what it means to "own" the phone call and to give not just good customer service, but *great* customer service—*Service that will amaze you*. My team does this by truly caring and having empathy for your situation. They are genuinely trying to help you solve whatever issue you may be having, whether it's general maintenance on your vehicle, a major repair, or an electronic problem. At Parkway Automotive, you'll meet people with the technology and the empathy to get answers for you.

After that, you'll discover that our philosophy on auto service is proactive. As we continue to monitor your vehicle's condition by having regular check-ups by an ASE Certified technician, we are going to know ahead of time the things that need attention immediately, and notify you of the things coming up to keep you and your family safe on the road. We provide this service through our **VIP Club** where you can purchase a club membership which entitles you to free oil changes, free tire rotations, and an inspection of your vehicle every 5,000 miles. It's fully transferrable from one car to the next without a transfer fee. You can find out more about our VIP Club at ParkwayAutomotive.net.

We also offer a **Two-Year Unlimited Mileage Warranty** on the work that we do. We're going to stand behind our work for that period of time, no questions asked.

Finally, we have a **100% Risk-Free, Money-Back Guarantee**. What we're telling you is that after we've made three attempts to repair your vehicle, if we have not repaired it to your satisfaction, we will give you 100% of your money back. There's absolutely no risk involved in having your car serviced at Parkway Automotive.

Let me assure you that when you bring your vehicle to Parkway, you'll experience the best of the best in Little Rock. In fact, we were voted "The Best of The Best in Little Rock" in 2012. We also received the "Ethics Award" from the Better Business Bureau, and in April 2012, I was featured on the cover of a national industry magazine, *Ratchet & Wrench*, and was recognized for being in the Top 2% of independent repair shops in the nation. Being chosen to receive these types of awards is a real honor for my team and me, and I hope gives you more confidence in choosing Parkway Automotive.

Giving Back to the Community

Please allow me to add some other thoughts that I think are important for you to know. It's so important for businesses to *give back,* and what we're really talking about *is people giving back to people.* Some of the ways that our company is involved and our people are giving back is through our support of the Arkansas Crisis Pregnancy Center. We support them by taking automobiles that people either can't or don't want to repair, and repairing them. We make them safe and then give them to the Crisis Pregnancy Center of Arkansas so that they can give them to their clients. This allows the Center to help moms who decide not to abort their children. These moms need help getting to the doctor, to work, and transporting their children to school. We can't do a lot, but this is one way we're able to contribute.

We also support a few elementary schools by giving back to the schools through the PTA. When a parent or grandparent has their vehicle serviced at Parkway Automotive, we give a portion back to their school PTA.

This assists the teachers with school supplies and other needs that benefit their students. Additionally, we recognize a "Teacher of the Month" at a local elementary school.

I also serve with Pulaski Technical College and on the Board of Directors for the Better Business Bureau of Arkansas. I believe it's important to be involved in the community and make sure people are having their needs met. A great community is not just about good business. It's about strong education in our schools as well. That's why I enjoy being involved and giving back in so many ways.

Something else I enjoy is being **Little Rock's only AAA Approved repair shop**. Everyone knows that AAA is an organization that can be trusted, and when they place their "stamp of approval" on something, you know it's been put through some tests.

Currently, Parkway Automotive is the only repair shop in Little Rock, including all of the local dealerships, that is approved by AAA Motor Club of North America. That says we meet their standards. And those standards are re-inspected every 12 months, both for our training and the certification of all our technicians, as well as for our service advisors and even the amount of insurance that we have. The lounge area must meet standards on how well it looks and how comfortable it is for our customers. All the services that an AAA member might expect, they will find when they come to Parkway Automotive.

There you have it — some of the background on Parkway Automotive and my philosophy of doing business. We really do want to provide outstanding customer service and help you solve any current issues, as well as assist you in maintaining your vehicle as long as you own it.

I know that our industry can be a bit confusing and very complex. Yet, at the same time, we all drive vehicles. I believe it's important for you to have at least a working knowledge of our industry and the terms we use so that you won't be taken advantage of unknowingly. In the following pages, I'll provide you with some helpful how-to's that can assist you in understanding the industry and your vehicle.

The rest of this book is less about me and more about you. I trust that you'll find it helpful!

Car Care 101

Acronyms

Communication can easily break down in my industry due to the many acronyms that we use. Listed here are some of the most common acronyms that you may hear and what they mean. I share them to give you a more thorough understanding which, I hope, will help you make more informed decisions in keeping your vehicle serviced properly.

LOF = Lube Oil and Filter Service

LOF is pronounced "loaf." What's a "loaf?" In our industry 'LOF' means Lube, Oil and Filter. Interestingly enough, not a lot of cars receive lubrication anymore, but the acronym has carried over for many, many years. So, if you see the term "LOF," that is basically talking about an oil change on a vehicle.

ABS = Anti-Lock Brake System

If you read that as a word, it says "abs." So, if we were a gym, you would think something totally different—one part of your body. But in the car industry, ABS is an acronym for Anti-lock Brake System. So, if your "ABS" light comes on, that means there's a fault in the Anti-lock Brake System. (*As far as your body is concerned, check with the gym on that!*)

DIS = Driver Information System

This is the vehicle's system that gives the driver information—in an LED type style, or scrolling across the dash or touch screen, or visible in a small window somewhere on the dash. This is a very important system on your vehicle that you need to be aware of. Pay attention to any message and look for specific responses in the index of your owner's manual.

CSS = Cooling System Service

CSS is our acronym for Cooling System Service. That's the process where we typically drain your cooling system and reinstall coolant. It's not a chemical flush; it's just a simple service of your cooling system fluid.

ASE = Automotive Service Excellence

You'll see this one a lot. ASE is an independent organization that tests the competency of those in our industry. ASE does not do training; they only do testing for competency. The training takes place in another location or through other venues, much like a student taking the SAT exam. It's administered at a testing location with a proctor and the results are provided by the certifying organization.

ASE says, "We're going to see if you learned anything through what you have studied. And if you can pass our test, then we will certify that you know what you are talking about and are qualified to repair these specific systems." When someone passes their exam they become "ASE Certified," and for the automotive repair side of our industry, there are eight different areas of ASE certification. If you are certified in all eight, you are an ASE Master Technician. I became Master certified (finally) in 2011.

ASE also has specific certifications for diesel trucks, like your light duty diesel. Additionally, they have certifications for heavy-duty diesel, certifications for people working in a parts department, and certifications for service advisors.

ASE is the "gold standard" in our industry, and in my opinion it is critical that anyone who works on your vehicle should be an ASE Certified technician. At Parkway, all of our technicians are ASE certified. In fact, we currently have three employees on staff who are ASE Master

Technicians. Additionally, our Service Advisors have ASE Certifications, which means that they understand your vehicle as well as the technician performing the work. Our Service Advisors can communicate this depth of knowledge to you in language that makes sense. This is an important distinction that you shouldn't overlook. Before you have any work done on your vehicle, ask if the person who will actually be doing the work is ASE Certified. If they aren't, you may want to look for a repair shop with fully trained and certified technicians and service advisors.

An interesting fact is that an ASE Certification has to be renewed every five (5) years. This is important because cars change and technology changes. So, ASE Certified Technicians are staying up to date on cutting edge technology so they can service your vehicles properly. Every year there are over a million pages of new information hitting our industry, so my technicians and I must always be reading and staying on top.

My great-grandfather said all he needed to fix his car was a piece of bailing wire, a pair of pliers and some duct tape. Today, we need a little more than that. That is why being ASE Certified is so important.

TPMS = Tire Pressure Monitoring System

TPMS stands for Tire Pressure Monitoring System. This system monitors the tire pressure of your car. After Ford had an escapade with low air pressure on their vehicles' tires causing numerous accidents, the federal government mandated that all vehicles, beginning in 2008/2009, must contain a Tire Pressure Monitoring System. Today, the technology actually notifies the driver when a tire has low pressure. Some systems will tell you a specific tire—for instance; your left front tire is low. Some will simply indicate that you have a low tire somewhere on the vehicle. Spare tires also have these sensors—so the four tires on the ground may be fine, but you should still check the spare tire.

EGR = Exhaust Gas Recirculation

EGR is one you'll hear often. It stands for Exhaust Gas Recirculation. It is an emission control item and a system that recirculates exhaust gases back into the engine for re-burning. Also, fumes from your gas tank make it back into the engine for re-burning through this system. All this has to do with fuel economy and your engine operating properly.

TPS = Throttle Position Sensor

In the recent past, your car had a physical cable that connected the gas pedal with the throttle control mechanism on the engine. Today, instead of a cable, your vehicle uses a throttle position sensor, which means that your actual gas pedal is now a sensor itself. So, when you are pushing down on the gas pedal, you are moving a sensor. The gas pedal sensor information is sent to the throttle position sensors, which tell the onboard computer how much gas and air to allow into the engine.

PCM = Powertrain Control Module

The PCM is the grandfather of the computer systems on the vehicle. It is the head honcho, the king, the president—it is what everything else goes through. Typically, there are many computers within a single car; they all must communicate with the PCM.

BCM = Body Control Module

The Body Control Module basically pays attention to everything internal (inside the vehicle). "Things that you touch" is a simple way to define what goes through the BCM. For example, your turn signals, your headlights, your heating and air controls, and others like these are all items that you touch. They all send information through the Body Control Module.

AT = Automatic Transmission

This is what most passenger vehicles have. If you move the gearshift from "Park" to "Reverse" or "Drive", then you have an Automatic Transmission. This type of transmission is designed to shift automatically when certain conditions exist. The invention of the automatic transmission revolutionized the driving of vehicles. Before this time they all had to be shifted into their different gears by the driver, using what we call a "manual" transmission.

Dashboard = Lights that pop up on the dashboard

As you sit in the driver's seat and turn on the key, you see all these lights that pop up on the dashboard. But what do they mean? First, there's a reason for the color of lights on your car dashboard. They can be associated with the red lights that you see when you are driving down the road.

If you see a RED light, what does that usually mean to you? Stop. And when you see YELLOW? Caution. GREEN? Green means go.

So let's apply this to the dashboard lights. If, for example, you have the cruise control on, the button is normally some sort of orange color. Once you set the cruise control, the button turns green.

Your dashboard lights are very important and should never be ignored. If one of your dashboard lights comes on, you need to have your vehicle serviced by a qualified technician.

ABS LIGHT = Anti-lock Brake System

The ABS light has to do with the brakes. If the ABS light is on, the Anti-lock Brake System computer has found a fault somewhere in the system. It could be anything from low brake fluid to a problem with a particular wheel sensor or another component within the system. When the ABS light is on, your normal braking will still work. However, if you get into a panic stop, the anti-lock brake system will *not* take over your braking—that is, your wheels will lock up like a normal vehicle not equipped with anti-lock brakes. So, you will lose the ability to maneuver around objects in your path. Instead, your momentum is going to carry you forward and you're probably going to hit the object ahead of you. You may remember your parents telling you that if you're on ice you should pump your brakes and not apply them hard. That principle is manifested in the ABS System. The ABS system pumps your brakes ten times per second, which is something no human is able to do.

The ABS light typically comes on as a red light. It doesn't mean that you have to immediately stop the car, but it does indicate to you that the system is not going to work until you get it resolved. So, you want to get it into a shop. It does not mean that your car won't stop; it does not mean that your brakes have failed completely; it only means that the anti-lock side of your brake system is not going to operate if you get into a panic stop situation. Drive cautiously—as you always should—and quickly get your vehicle to a shop for testing.

Check Engine Light

The check engine light has been around for many years. Since about 1990, it has evolved from its original purpose of simply giving information about the emission control status of the vehicle. Check engine lights are typically orange in color because they still primarily deal with emission controls. However, there are many more factors on today's vehicles which impact emissions that the government has determined are a part of emission controls.

Emissions concerns polluting the air—so, if there is a spark plug that is not firing the way it should, is not carrying electricity the way it should, is not burning fuel the way it is supposed to, and therefore is causing the car to pollute more than it should, the check engine light will come on. That's because of a government mandate that made the check engine light more comprehensive than it was originally.

Formerly, if you had a failed spark plug you wouldn't see the check engine light come on. The check engine light would come on if you had a fuel canister that was full of gasoline or if the EGR (Exhaust Gas Recirculation, remember) system failed. But now, the check engine light encompasses so many things; there are somewhere between six hundred and nine hundred different reasons why the check engine light might come on. That's why just having a code read doesn't do you much good—that only tells you which system may be at fault. At that point, a technician needs to run tests on the specific system to determine the actual cause so they can correct this problem.

SRS Light

Air bags are very important. The air bag system is similar to the ABS system in that if the light is on, the air bag is not going to work properly if you're in an accident. In a car equipped with air bags you will see an SRS light (or Air Bag light) on the dashboard. *SRS is an acronym for Supplementary Restraint System*—the key word being "supplementary." That means that it is a supplementing part of a safety system, and that safety system is your seat belt. If you are not wearing your seat belt and you are in an accident that deploys the airbags, then a greater amount of bodily injury will occur. So, for that reason, **you should always wear your seatbelt**. If the airbag light is on, that means that the airbags will not deploy if an accident occurs—there is a problem in the system. In order to prevent your airbags from deploying on their own, there are many safety features in place to ensure they don't come out unless there is an accident. However, if the SRS light is on, you definitely want to get that tested to find out what is at fault. *If the SRS light is on, your airbags will not deploy in an accident.*

Traction Control Light

The vehicle computer not only monitors the brake system, it also helps move power from one tire to another in all-wheel-drive vehicles. For example, say you are in an all-wheel drive vehicle. You are stuck on ice or in snow and you are trying to get out. One of your wheels is usually stuck worse than the others—it's spinning but not getting any traction. The traction control system will move the power from the wheel that is spinning to a wheel that is not merely spinning, since the non spinning wheel has greater traction. The traction control system allows power to be transferred so that you can gain traction and have greater control and get out of a situation where you may normally be stuck.

Traction control is also working during acceleration. An example of acceleration mode is when you are turning a corner and the weight of the car gets distributed from one side to the other. The traction control system is going to move the power to the wheel that has the best traction.

The traction control light comes on momentarily whenever the traction control system activates. If there's a failure in the system then the light will come on and stay on. Typically, traction control lights are yellow, not red. So if the traction light comes on for a moment as you are accelerating or as a wheel is spinning and then turns off again, you don't need to take your vehicle in. However, if the light comes on and stays on, that's indicative of an issue within that system. That is when you need to take your vehicle for inspection.

Reduced Power Light

Reduced power is something that is primarily seen on GM vehicles. The reduced power light is usually red and indicates that something has gone wrong, that the vehicle has gone into "limp mode"—as in "we are limping" or "we only have one leg and cannot run." There is some fault that the system has found that could potentially be problematic. A lot of times this fault deals with either transmission functions or accelerating functions. So, the vehicle goes into limp mode, the reduced power light comes on, and you have to get it in for service. You can drive to get yourself to a safe place; however, some limp modes would limit you to driving no more than 25 miles an hour—where of course you would want to have it towed from that point if you have a long way to go. Other limp modes may allow you to go 40 miles per hour, enough that you can get to a repair facility on your own. The reduced power light will most always be red. It indicates a problem that needs to receive immediate attention.

Temperature Light

Most cars today have an engine temperature gauge as well as a temperature light. The engine temperature light will always be red—indicating that you need to shut the car down as soon as possible. The longer you continue to drive, the more damage will occur. Eventually, you will damage the engine internally. By continuing to drive the vehicle, you will create more problems—very costly problems. **When the temperature light comes on, you should pull over and turn the engine off as quickly as you safely can.** When the temperature light comes on, you should immediately look at the temperature gauge. If the gauge is too hot, you need to shut your car off as soon as possible. The first step in the troubleshooting process is to make sure that your coolant level is full. *But be careful!* You have to use extreme caution when adding coolant to a car that is hot because you can get burned. It is best to let the car sit for several hours and cool down before adding coolant.

Whenever you have to add coolant to your car, that means you have a leak that needs serviced. If the coolant is full and the vehicle is running hot, then that means that a component within the system has failed.

Oil Light

The oil light can indicate an issue with the oil level or oil pressure—sometimes both. If the engine loses oil pressure, the oil light is going to come on. That light will be red because you have to shut the engine down quickly. If the oil pressure is too low, there will be internal damage to the engine. The damage would be similar to driving without oil in the engine.

To clarify, you can be low on oil and still have oil pressure. The oil light may not let you know that you are low on oil—in some cars only checking the dipstick can tell you that you are low on oil. There is some new technology in some of the higher end cars, the BMWs and Mercedes models, where there is no dipstick. Instead, there is a sensor inside the engine that reads the oil level and indicates whether the oil is low or if the oil is at the proper level. However, that is a very small percentage of the cars that are on the market today. Most cars still have a dipstick. You can actually be a quart or even two quarts low on oil but still have enough oil in the engine to produce oil pressure. In that case, the oil light might not come on because the oil pressure is there—so, that part of the system might never give you an indication that you're low on oil. Obviously, if you have no oil, you will not have any oil pressure at all. At that point, you've probably damaged the engine. That is why it is important to inspect a vehicle's oil level periodically.

Having a sufficient oil level provides several benefits. Lubricating the engine is the oil's primary job, but outside of that the biggest impact that oil has is on fuel mileage. That's why the weights of oil have changed over the years—car manufacturers have learned that if they use just the right oil then they can improve fuel mileage, perhaps by 1/10th of 1%. In some cases, that small amount is enough to help the manufacturer meet the federal guidelines for fuel economy.

Smart Air Bag Light

Almost all cars are equipped with smart air bags. Basically, these sensors measure the weight of the passenger in the front passenger seat. *Fortunately, there is not an electronic display on the dash of your weight!* Depending on the weight of the person or object that is in the passenger front seat, the air bag may or may not deploy. With this light, there is not necessarily anything that you need to do. If there is a small child in the front seat the smart bag knows it. If the weight in the front seat does not meet a certain criterion that has been established by the manufacturer, then the smart air bag light will come on to let you know that the airbag is off on the passenger side.

Through some unfortunate deaths and injuries over the years, the car industry has learned that some small children's bodies cannot withstand the explosion of an airbag. On the inside of an airbag is a substance that is basically gunpowder. When triggered, the "gunpowder" explodes the bag out of the dash at an extremely high rate of speed. The air that is in that bag immediately deflates, but is present for just long enough to provide a cushion. Typically, the occupant of the seat is moving forward while the bag is deploying rearward, so there is a collision that takes place between the bag and the occupant. Because the airbag deploys at such a high rate of speed, if the body of the person in the front seat is not big enough to handle the rearward movement of the airbag or the explosion that deploys the airbag then the airbag will cause bodily injury. Most people who have experienced an airbag deployment will have some facial scratches or contusions somewhere on their face from that airbag deploying. However, these are superficial and not major. But with a small child, the airbag's rapid deployment could break the child's neck or back or cause a head injury. After learning this, car manufacturers introduced smart bags. *Which was smart!*

Dashboard Gauges

Many cars have not only dashboard lights but also dashboard gauges. They are there to help us know how the vehicle is operating.

Temperature Gauge

One very common gauge is the cold/hot gauge, also called the coolant temperature gauge. Typically, you will find the coolant temperature gauge on the left side of the dash. This

gauge was mentioned earlier, but to summarize, it is

basically monitoring the temperature of the engine. Transmissions usually will not shift into the final drive gear until the engine temperature has reached at least a quarter of the way of its full gauge range. Most gauges are set to run—in normal operation—about midway up the gauge. So, you'll usually see a "C" on the bottom and an "H" on the top (or Blue for cold and Red for hot). The gauge could also be horizontally installed—in that case the 'C' would be on the left and the 'H' would be on the right. The needle is typically going to be in the middle of the gauge, indicating what is called Operating Temperature.

Interestingly, if the indicator needle stays over on the cold side, then that impacts your fuel mileage. That's because the vehicle's computer is designed to put fuel in the engine based on a certain engine temperature. When the engine is cold, it puts in more fuel because a cold engine needs more fuel. If the thermostat is not working— the typical failure—then the computer perceives that the engine is running at a colder temperature and will continue putting more fuel into the engine. Thus, you will use more gasoline. So, because the thermostat can impact fuel mileage, it is important that you are familiar with the temperature gauge to know what is normal. It is all about checking that gauge on a consistent basis. *Remember that continuing to run the vehicle when the gauge shows the engine is hot will cause expensive internal engine damage.*

Tachometer

Most tachometer gauges (also called RPM gauges) are circular and have a series of numbers going around them—often 0-7.

As you depress the gas pedal, even if you are sitting still, you will see the tachometer needle move around the gauge as you accelerate. The tachometer indicates how many times the engine is rotating each minute. You multiply the number on the gauge by one thousand—for example, if the needle is sitting at 1, the engine is rotating one thousand times per minute. If the numbers on the tachometer are multiples of 10—numbers like 20, 30, 40, and so on—then you multiply that number by one hundred instead of one thousand. That number is how many times the engine is making one full revolution each minute—called revolutions per minute or "RPM" for short.

It can be helpful to keep an eye on the RPM gauge. The RPM number will drop each time the transmission shifts into a higher gear to increase fuel economy. If you see that the engine appears to be running at a higher RPM than normal, that is an indication that something is not right because the engine is working harder than it usually does. Fundamentally, the tachometer measures the speed of the engine in revolutions per minute.

Another place the tachometer is helpful is when you are idling. If you have a vacuum leak or a similar problem, your idling RPM will be higher than usual. Most engines should run just below the 1 mark—or possibly the 10, depending on what kind of gauge you have. If the idling RPM is significantly higher, that's a problem. You should expect to see the idling RPM a little bit higher when the engine is cold. Once the engine reaches operating temperature you will see the gauge go back down to the 650-750 RPM range. *Isn't it cool that you already understand acronyms?*

Battery Gauge

The battery gauge simply measures battery voltage. You will usually see a small picture of what looks like a battery. It can make you aware when there is a problem with the battery. Some gauges will have a number 12, which concerns the voltage, but most of the time the normal position for the needle, when everything is fine with the battery, is in the middle of the gauge.

Fuel Gauge

Most people know that "E" does not stand for "enough"—it stands for empty. And "F" of course stands for full.

In today's cars, the fuel pump is located *inside* the gas tank. Having enough fuel in the tank helps keep that little electric motor—called your fuel pump—cool, and will typically make it last longer. So, just <u>as a general rule, you should keep at least a quarter tank of fuel in your car at all times</u>. This will add life to the fuel pump because, since it is an electric motor, it does create heat, and excessive heat causes the pump to have a shorter life. So keeping enough fuel in the tank will keep the fuel pump cool and will simply help it last longer.

If you get down to a quarter tank, you can let it go down to empty—it is OK to do that—but when you fill up you should fill up all the way. You shouldn't put just a couple of dollars worth of gas in where the fuel level just reaches a quarter. If you're always running in that quarter to empty range, then you're going to shorten the life of the pump. Not only that, but also if there's an emergency and you need to get somewhere right away, you will want more than a quarter tank of gas in the car. So using a quarter tank as your empty gauge would be a good rule of thumb so that you can lengthen the life of the fuel pump and get you where you need to go in an emergency.

Odometer

The odometer gauge tells you how many miles are on your vehicle. The accuracy of an odometer gauge has changed over the years. Today it's electronic—whereas years ago there used to be a cable that ran from the speedometer head down to the transmission. As the transmission rotated, this cable would rotate. You would be able to take that cable out, put a drill on it, run the drill backwards, and reduce the miles on the car. That was an unethical trick from the '50s and the '60s, but nowadays that's impossible. You cannot run mileage back on a car; it is completely electronic. Almost all odometers are LED displayed at some level, and so there's not any type of manipulation that can occur for someone to show fewer miles on the car than it actually has. The odometer gauge is an accurate way for you to know how many miles are on a car.

Speedometer

The speedometer gauge is, of course, useful for knowing how fast you are going. It has speed sensors that are very accurate. That information is used for the transmission, to let it know when to shift. *Of course, it is also hopefully there to keep you from getting a speeding ticket.*

These are the primary gauges you'll find on the dashboard of vehicles today. Not all vehicles will have all of these gauges, but you should be familiar with each of them so that you'll know how to properly read the gauge when you see it.

Noises

One of the greatest things about car ownership is really getting to know your car. That means using your five senses—hearing, sight, smell, taste, and touch. You can use your senses to know what is normal on the car so you'll recognize when something has changed.

When it comes to hearing noises that you know are not normal, not what you are used to hearing, one of the best things to do is "show the noise."

When you take the car into a service facility, don't try to explain the noise, show them the noise. One of the greatest helps to any service facility is when the vehicle owner pays attention so they can duplicate the noise.

- How fast was I going?

- Was I turning?

- Was I braking?

- Was I accelerating?

- What were the scenarios?

- Was I going uphill or downhill?

Pay attention to the environment and the activity that is taking place when the noise occurs. Then you can take that information, go to the repair facility, get someone in the car with you and duplicate the sound. Highly trained automotive technicians can typically hear many noises that you may not hear. This small step will assist the technician in locating and correcting the same noise that concerned you. When you pay attention to how the car normally sounds, when something changes you'll know it.

Brake Squeaking

One very common noise that often scares people is a squeaky noise that happens when you push on your brake pedal. If you hear a high-pitched noise, that is certainly indicative of brakes needing repair, especially if it is something that you have not normally heard. Sometimes what we'll call "inferior" brake pads or "inferior" parts can be used on a brake job. In those cases, you should expect some squeaking. What is happening is not necessarily metal contacting metal, but actually a vibration of the brake pad against the rotor, which comes out as an audible squeak. The vibration is at a decibel level that sounds like a squeak, so this can occur due to the type of brake pad being used or the surface of the rotor. However, if you have good brake systems and high quality parts being used in the brakes, you should not expect to hear any noise. If noise does occur at some point in the future, you should recognize it as a problem and have the brake system inspected for any wear, tear, or other issue.

Brake Grinding

Grinding usually happens after squeaking, but I have also seen some brakes that did not squeak and went right to grinding. That is typically metal grinding on metal, and you definitely need to get your vehicle into a shop. Some of the higher end manufacturers, such as Mercedes, BMW and Lexus, will have what are called "brake pad wear indicators." These are just a small wire that is built into the brake pad. Once that wire makes contact with the rotor, a dash light comes on that says "brake wear indicator." At that point, you can bet that it is time to replace your pads. Once the sensor makes contact with the rotor, the sensor is ruined and will have to be replaced along with the brake pads.

Squeaky Engine

Many times you'll find a plastic splash shield that is installed underneath the front of the car for multiple purposes. They are there not only to prevent foreign objects like rocks from getting into the engine compartment and causing damage, but also to protect against water getting into the drive belt area. If water has entered that area, many times the drive belt is actually slipping on the pulleys. You are hearing the squeaking noise because water intrusion has occurred. This is not really harmful but it probably does mean that the shield that is normally present is either disfigured in some way or not there at all.

Those shields get damaged frequently when you pull up close to parking spots and hit the sidewalk curb slightly, or when you hit one of those parking stops because your car sits a little bit lower. If you hit that shield enough times, eventually it is not going to stay attached and will come off. That's a bad situation because your lower engine area is now exposed and could sustain damage from a rock or other debris. You should look to see if this plastic shield is in good condition when you wash your car or get fuel. It only takes a moment and could save you thousands of dollars in repairs.

Thumping While Turning

Sometimes when you turn, you will get a thumping noise and possibly a jerking action through the steering wheel. A thumping noise can be caused by several problems. It could be caused by what are called your "constant velocity joints" or CV joints. Your axle has a constant velocity joint built into it that maintains quickness of motion to the wheels when you turn your steering wheel. When CV joints wear out, they will cause a thumping or knocking noise when you turn. The only repair option is to replace the axle itself.

Another thumping that can occur involves the brakes. Usually occurring at highway speeds, you will apply the brakes and get a thumping noise. It may be something you hear or something you feel. Many times you will see the steering wheel shake. That usually means that the rotors, which are a brake component, are out of round.

Those rotors turn with the wheel as you are driving. When you apply the brakes, the brake pads rub against the rotor to create the friction that causes your vehicle to slow down. If the surface of the rotor is not smooth or straight, it produces a thumping or a vibration. Another term used is **"pulsation of the brakes"** when you apply them. Typically, you will hear or feel that pulsation when you brake at speeds above 45 miles per hour. You may not necessarily feel the pulsations if you are braking at 20 miles per hour, but once you get up to highway speeds and apply the brakes, you are more likely to feel or hear the vibrations. This is not necessarily a dangerous situation but can be quite a nuisance. It also has a negative impact on brake pad and suspension life.

Thumping While Driving

If you are driving down the road and getting a regular thumping or vibration that varies with your speed, the tires are definitely the place to check. Many times, what we'll see is the tread in the tire separating internally. To be accurate, "see" is not the best word because it is not something you can see because separation of the tread occurs on the inside of the tire. The tread will move or separate slightly. The symptom that alerts you that this has occurred more times than not is this:

If you are driving across a parking lot at 2-3 miles per hour—a really slow speed—and let go of the steering wheel, your steering wheel will shake back and forth, slightly left to right. That is a good indication that the tread has moved inside the tire, and you will definitely want to have the tires replaced.

The age at which you should replace a tire has become an issue over the years. All tires have a number on them that indicates the age of the tire. You can find one of those numbers on every tire. The number will start with the letters DOT (an abbreviation for Department of Transportation) and followed by a series of letters and numbers. At the end of that series will be four digits. Those digits represent the week and year that the tire was made. If one of your tires has the digits 4512, the tire was made in the 45th week of 2012. The numerical significance is that the recommendation for replacing tires is between five and seven years old. If the tires are 10 years old, it is absolutely required that you replace the tires. I say it is "required" because you are at a great risk of a blow out or tire separation when a tire is that old.

Whining Engine

Whining usually occurs either from the children in the back seat or from the car's steering pump under the hood. So you want to check both of those. You may need a cracker for one and power steering fluid for the other.

The power steering fluid is a sealed system for the most part. The fluid does not wear out or go away. If you need to add power steering fluid, you most likely have a leak somewhere in the system. Typically, if you add power steering fluid you should expect the whine to come back because of a leak somewhere. It may not even go away after you add the fluid because you have to make some turning maneuvers to help work the new fluid through the system. The whine may stop for a while, but once the fluid leaks out again, the whining noise will begin again.

Interestingly enough, as Ford power steering pumps get older, whining is normal for them. The whining is not loud, but it will be present and it is likely to be something you hear. If everything is sealed, there is no loss of fluid. If the fluid has been flushed out and changed regularly, then it is not abnormal to hear those older pumps whine. To be safe, if you hear a whining noise, after checking the kids in the back seat, consider having your power steering system checked by a certified technician.

Vehicle Starting

When you start your car, there are several noises that you could hear. One is a tapping noise that can indicate that your oil is not getting where it needs to be. That noise occurs because some areas of the car need to have oil immediately upon starting. One reason that some of the manufacturers have gone to a lighter weight oil is because that oil can get to those areas that need lubrication quicker on start-up more rapidly.

Another noise you might hear is a rattling. Any time you hear a rattle in your engine when you start your car, it is metal-to-metal contact. While it will not cause immediate failure, it is something that will eventually happen. That is going to take its toll on the engine over time. Usually, this is an indication that you are low on oil.

Alternatively, it could also be an indication that you do not have the oil pressure that you need, or even that internal wear has occurred.

Engine Oil

Here are some common questions about engine oil:

- *Does the type of engine oil I put in really matter?*

- *Can I change the brand of oil that I use?*

- *What do the numbers mean?*

Engine Oil Background

All oil today is what is called "paraffin-based oil." That means the oil has the ability to capture dirt—this is its job. When the time for service comes, the oil is drained out of the vehicle and dirt goes with it. No matter what oil you are using, it is all paraffin-based and it is used to remove dirt from the engine at each service interval.

That being said, the manufacturers have made different changes within the oil for their specific engine to bring about the kind of lubrication that is needed. This goes back to the tolerances that are built within the engine, and affects fuel mileage. It used to be that the car industry would recommend oil based on geographic conditions. If you lived in Alaska where it is really cold, thinner winter oil would be recommended. If you lived in the warmer southern states, something else would be recommended. That has all changed because of the tolerances that have been built into cars by the manufacturers. Today it is more important than ever that you pay attention to what type of oil the manufacturer is recommending. Some European car manufacturers are advising that you have to use full synthetic oil. In some cases they will tell you to use Mobile 1 oil in your car, which is the world's leading synthetic motor oil.

In 2011, General Motors put out a standard called "dexos." Dexos oil was actually General Motors' attempt to brand their own oil and require it to be used in their cars. There has been a lot of controversy over that because it is actually a type of monopoly, but there are other people a lot smarter than me involved in that conversation. General Motors has said that for some engines, not using dexos approved oil or dexos equivalent could hurt performance and even cause engine damage. If you use fully synthetic oil, then it is dexos equivalent, because that's basically what dexos oil is.

If you look at an oil bottle you will see all kinds of information on it. Probably, the one thing that most people see more than anything is the 5W30 or 10W30. What does that mean? Well, the "W" stands for winter. If we used 5W30 for example, the "5" and "30" actually measure the thickness of the oil at different temperatures. If an oil bottle has "5W30" on it, in winter climates the oil has a viscosity of 30. Once the oil heats up, it has a viscosity of "5." Most cars today use either 5W20 or 5W30, and you want to use the specified oil regardless of geographic location. The brand you choose is up to you. Contrary to what your grandfather told you its ok to switch brands.

Oil Change Frequency

How often you should change your oil is becoming an issue in our industry because of changes in service intervals. "Whenever the oil needs changed" has always been the standard for people to know to bring their car in for service. Years ago it was three months or three thousand miles. Our fathers, grandfathers, and great-grandfathers all taught us that. The reason the oil needed changed so often is because the engines were exposed to the elements, and the filtering system of air and fuel was just not what it is today. Your oil could be contaminated very easily and cause internal engine damage. That is also why car engines used to last only about fifty thousand miles. Several things have changed since then. First, as I mentioned earlier, the oil has gotten better at suspending dirt. With the advent of electronic fuel injection, we do not have as much of a problem with the outside elements making it to the crankcase because the fuel systems are sealed. Fuel is also being managed better, so the oil is not getting contaminated with fuel the way it used to.

We are getting better control of the outside elements of dirt and dust coming into the engine; we have better control through better filtering. We have better control of the amount of fuel that gets dumped into an engine for burning—almost all of it is getting burned these days. And finally, the oil has gotten better at suspending the dirt in the engine. When you put these three factors into the equation, your service interval can now be a lot longer than it used to be. Some manufacturers will tell you 7,500 miles, some 10,000 miles, and some 15,000 miles. To help simplify things, a lot of cars today have oil life monitors on them that tell you when it is time to change your oil.

A general rule of thumb that I have adopted is:

Your oil should be serviced every 5,000 miles.

The reason I landed on five thousand miles is primarily because that is the interval at which several other aspects of the car need to be inspected. For example, the tires should be rotated then. The car ought to be inspected by an ASE Certified Technician at that interval to make sure everything else is working safely and properly. That is also a good time to change the oil. *This is the interval at which you receive free oil changes as a VIP Member at Parkway Automotive.*

Some manufacturers have made these long recommendations for oil changes, only to find out that the extended duration caused internal engine damage or failure for the consumer after seventy, eighty, or ninety thousand miles. Too late, they realized that they should have had that interval a little closer. Changing the oil every five thousand miles is a good rule of thumb.

Oil suspends dust particles in a manner like a dust rag that you would use in your home. The oil will collect the dust and debris that is in your engine, but that same oil is still going through the system. If you don't change the oil on a regular basis, all of those particles are still going through your engine. That's one of the reasons that you need to get it out of your engine on a regular basis—so you have a fresh dust cloth, per se.

Car Care 201

In this section let's go over some of the more advanced areas of your vehicle, including when to buy a new one. This could become a reference manual for you and a great training manual for new drivers you may have in your family. I've structured this section in the form of a Question and Answer series, much like an FAQ section of a website or resource book.

Buying A New Car

Let's discuss a few of the most frequently questions related to purchasing a new vehicle. Having this information could save you thousands of dollars.

When to Buy a Newer Vehicle

Q. When do I need to buy a new car versus investing in the one I have?

A. Every car has a point of diminishing return. What you do from the day you drive your car off the showroom floor and whether you think of your vehicle as an investment or expense will impact the decisions you make when it comes time for you to consider replacing it.

You should not say, "Well, I don't want to put that much money in my car." If you've maintained the car well, if you've been a part of our VIP club membership and we've serviced your car every 5,000 miles, if you've taken care of things properly, then you should expect to get 300,000 to 400,000 miles from it. The car will last you that long if you are caring for it correctly. That is one of the reasons you see Hondas and Toyotas last so long. It's not necessarily because of the car, but rather because the people who buy them take care of them. If you'll do the same with your Ford, Chevy, Chrysler, or other vehicle, you can expect to get a lot of miles out of them as well: they are all quality vehicles. When you buy a vehicle, you have to understand that <u>how you maintain it today is going to impact its condition tomorrow</u>. With proper servicing, your point of diminishing returns is going to be a lot farther down the road than if you allow it to be neglected.

I have seen vehicles with as few as 75,000 miles on them that need an engine because the oil was not changed properly. Today, that is a $7,000 to $10,000 venture, and depending on the vehicle, that car may not be worth it. If, however, you have it financed and you owe money on it and you're "upside down" (meaning you owe more than the vehicle is worth), then sometimes you don't have a choice.

It is always better to maintain a car correctly from the beginning so that the point of diminishing returns is much farther out than it otherwise would be.

Say you have a six or seven-year-old vehicle. Maybe it needs a timing belt or has blown a head gasket. It is going to be a $1,500 to $2,500 repair on a vehicle that you have been driving for six to seven years. You know the vehicle, but you are just not sure you want to pay that much to get it fixed. You think you might just want to buy a newer vehicle. I have done a calculation that can help you decide. It explains that it is not always in your best interests not to repair it but to buy a different vehicle.

Larry Burkett was a well-known financial advisor who started Crown Financial Ministries. He would tell you that the cheapest car you will ever own is the one in your driveway. What he means is that by having the car maintained and having everything in order, you will still spend less money having the repair made than purchasing a newer vehicle.

When we talk about making a major repair on a car, a way that you can try to crunch the numbers is to ask yourself, "What's it going to cost me over the next year?"

Let's say there is $3,000 worth of work that needs to be done on your vehicle and you have decided you are not going to repair it. Instead, you are going to go buy a used vehicle. Even if you bought a rather cheap car, say it was $10,000. First you would have the sales tax. Currently, in Arkansas, that's 9% or $900. You're still going to have some depreciation off the vehicle of somewhere between $500 and $1,000 in a very short period of time after buying it. Your personal property taxes will go up. Your insurance will increase because if you finance the car, you'll have to have full coverage insurance. Look at what's going to be your total outgo over the next 12 months for the car that's sitting in front of you versus purchasing a used car.

The monthly payments on a $10,000 car would be around $200 over a period of 12 months or $2,400. Add $900 for the sales tax and you are now at $3,250 for the first year, plus depreciation and we haven't done anything to maintain the car yet. So, if you apply that same principle to a brand new car, these dollar figures are going to go up exponentially. Almost always, it makes sense to fix your existing older car rather than to buy a new one.

If you just repair your existing car, you'll probably have enough money to make your old car look like new with wax jobs, full details, or improvements. I know a lot of people who drive old cars that look really, really good (Refer to the front cover of this book).

Extended Warranties

Q: *If I buy a new vehicle, should I buy an extended warranty?*

A: First, extended warranties are all over the board. When you go into the dealership to buy an extended warranty, they typically offer two types. One is the type that the manufacturer offers, so if I bought a Ford, it would be a Ford extended warranty. If I bought a GM, it would be a GM extended warranty. The dealership will typically sell a manufacturer's extended warranty and they will also have available what is called an "after-market extended warranty." That is usually from a company whose sole product is extended warranties.

For whatever reason, most after-market extended warranty companies have been located or were started in the St. Louis area. I'll just tell you that the St. Louis Better Business Bureau and the St. Louis Attorney General spend a lot of time dealing with these companies because of complaints from consumers who have purchased these warranties. Probably the biggest complaint of all concerning extended warranties is believing that something is covered, and when it comes time for that to be replaced, you find out it is not covered.

ConsumerAffairs.com says,

"From what we've heard, we suspect that most extended warranties are a waste of money that could be better spent on performing exquisite maintenance, still the best insurance of trouble-free motoring."

They also said, "Sixty-five percent (or more than 8,000) **Consumer Reports** readers surveyed by the Consumer Reports National Research Center earlier in the winter of 2011 said they spent significantly more for a new car warranty than they got back in repair cost savings." That is very common.
(http://www.consumeraffairs.com/news04/2005/extended_warranty.html)

There are even conventions to determine how to sell you an extended warranty. The information that I'm about to give you is from the website, *WarrantyInnovations.com*.

The whole purpose of the convention, throughout all their breakout sessions and their main course, was this—and this is in the notes of the meeting!

"The discussion will also include ways to leverage systems and data to drive extended warranty sales, how to build a recurring revenue stream with extended warranties in maintenance, lower costs,

and claims against your program and how to better work with your insurance and our administrator."

That information clearly states that their intent is to sell more warranties and reduce the number of claims. Extended warranties are a contract, and I learned a long time ago that contracts are written in favor of those who write them.

<u>Without question, extended warranty contracts are not good for the consumer.</u> Can you find people who have been able to save money in buying an extended warranty? Yes, you can. The response rate according to *Consumer Reports* is about one in five—so about 20% said they had a net savings.

The *Consumer Reports* study basically said that when you're buying, it is better not to buy an extended warranty, but instead use those dollars to maintain your vehicle. In the survey, respondents cited warranty costs of $1,000 on average that provided benefits of $700—a $300 loss. Forty-two percent of extended warranties were never used, and only about a third of all respondents used their plan to cover a serious problem.

There are also some things that are not covered by an extended warranty. So, even though you purchased the warranty, you're still going to have to pay for some repairs that are not covered by the warranty because there is a lot of fine print in them. There will be things like fluids (e.g., transmission fluid) that they won't pay for.

<u>Most extended warranties give the warranty company the option of putting a used part on your car.</u> So if your transmission goes out, instead of getting a new

transmission, you could get a used one—one out of a salvage yard or from a recycler. That is the option extended warranty companies have. It's their choice, not yours. That's scary, but it saves them money, and many times that is what they choose to do. As I have mentioned, contracts are written in favor of those who write them.

Caring for your Car

Q. When should I jump start my car?

A. The purpose of a battery is to turn the engine over to start the car. It will not be the cause of the engine failing while driving or even shutting off while driving. The typical time that you expect to jump start a car is when something happens when you're initially trying to start the engine. There is no noise, or maybe there are repetitive clicks, but the engine does not turn over—it does not crank or "turn over," as we say. The job of the starter is to turn the engine over, and the starter gets its power to do that from the battery. That is the only job for the battery.

If you're driving down the road and your car dies, the battery is not the cause of your car dying. That is not the time to jump start your car. It will not fix it. I've seen people in the middle of intersections trying to jump start their car, and they would not be in that intersection if the battery was the problem, simply because that would not be the reason it died or quit running. So the only time you need to jump start your vehicle is when it will not crank over.

Note: *See the "How-To" Section to learn the proper way to jump start your car should you have the need.*

Premium Fuel

Q. Do I need to buy premium fuel? What is it, and what does it do? What is the return on investment for buying premium fuel?

A. The best way to determine if premium fuel is right for you is to actually check your gas mileage. When it comes down to the question, "Do I have to buy premium fuel?" you would want to take a look at the owner's manual of your automobile to see if it actually has that requirement. Typically what you will see is that the requirement will be on your high-end vehicles — BMWs, Mercedes, and some Lexus vehicles. The owner's manual will tell you to put in only the premium fuel. The reason for that requirement is that the vehicle has been designed in such a way to burn fuel at the optimum levels. Both the way the engine is timed and tuned and the type of spark plugs used, mean that if you burn a higher-grade fuel or a higher octane rating then you will get the optimum performance out of your vehicle.

So there is nothing wrong with using 87% octane. The engine will automatically change the timing on that vehicle for that gas so that it will burn that fuel without the engine pinging or what's called "labor knocking." A component put in vehicles a few years ago was called "knock sensors." Knock sensors adjust the timing if the engine begins to "ping" or "knock" as a result of low octane or other factors in the fuel. **So do you have to use premium fuel? The answer is absolutely not**—you do not have to use it. But if you want the best performance and the best fuel mileage for the way that car was built, then it would be recommended to use the higher-grade gasoline.

The return on investment is simply a crunching of the numbers. You should go through three to five gas tanks full of fuel, measuring your fuel mileage, and then make a decision if premium fuel is right for you. We all know that fuel mileage depends on how heavy your right foot is, the driving conditions, environmental conditions, and more. You would just have to crunch some numbers. Usually I would run three to five tanks of regular fuel and then three to five tanks on the higher octane, and then make an informed decision: "Is it really helping me?"

Lifetime Preventative Maintenance Plans

Q. How much does car maintenance cost? Is it better to proactively keep cars maintained or wait until they break down? What will save me the most money long-term?

A. **Consumer Reports** did a report that came out in 2012 concerning the percent of cost of owning a vehicle in a one-year, a three-year, a five-year, and an eight-year time frame, and they determined how a percentage of total dollars is spent. There are six areas in which you spend money on a car:

1. Depreciation

2. Fuel

3. Interest rate (e.g. having the car financed)

4. Insurance

5. Taxes

6. Maintenance and repair

When we talk about maintenance and repair, what is interesting is that only 1% of the total cost of your vehicle the first year of ownership is attributed to maintenance and repair. Most cars are, of course, under warranty, so there would not be any type of repair, simply primary maintenance. Looking at the three-year number, it goes to 2%, on the five-year it goes to 4% of total cost, and an eight-year-old vehicle, you can expect the total cost of maintenance and repair to be about 6% of your total cost of owning that vehicle per year.

So, as you can see, we would expect that to grow as a car gets older, so what you want to look for is a maintenance plan. Some manufacturers sell what is called a PPM, or a Prepaid Maintenance Plan. A lot of times they will sell those to you when you buy the car, and they roll it into the cost of the vehicle. That may be convenient, but it is also the most costly way that you could ever pay for maintenance —to prepay it when you are financing the automobile. Imagine paying interest on car maintenance!

That's exactly what you are doing when you finance a maintenance plan.

Other dealers and manufacturers are actually selling a maintenance plan that you can buy within the service lane of the dealership—typically a one-year, a three-year, or a five-year plan. With it, you get a package of services inside a specific amount of time. So typically, if I bought the one-year plan, I would have three oil changes within that one-year plan, and no matter what, I can get all three oil changes within that one year regardless of the mileage. It is based solely on time frame. That is pretty typical with dealers.

What we've created at Parkway Automotive—what we believe with respect to prepaid maintenance—is that we have a **Lifetime VIP Program**. As a Parkway VIP, you pay one price for the plan and it's good for as long as you are living and we are in business. **A major difference from the PPMs is that <u>ours will transfer</u> to a replacement vehicle at no additional cost**. So, you can actually transfer the membership to the next vehicle and never pay a renewal or transfer fee. <u>As a Parkway VIP you'll receive FREE Oil Changes for Life, a vehicle inspection, tire rotations and a discount on labor service.</u>

We believe that a car should have the oil changed about every 5,000 miles, have the tires rotated every 5,000 miles, as well as a good inspection completed by an ASE Certified technician. We have a light inspection done at 5,000 miles, and then a major inspection done at 10,000, and then another light one at 15,000, and then a major one at 20,000—so, every 10,000 miles an ASE technician is doing a major inspection of your car, including a test drive for his expertise to determine if everything is okay. Then you get a full report. We believe that if we can do a good inspection on your car—with the major inspection every 10,000 miles—and the technician is making a good report on the car, then you are going to be able to avoid most breakdowns and a whole lot of repair costs. The fluids in your car are cheaper than the parts that they protect, so by having those fluids replaced at regular intervals, you are going to save money on repairs.

This philosophy helped us to develop our VIP club membership where we inspect your vehicle, keep you informed of any repair issues, inspect how your brakes are wearing, and any safety or maintenance items on your car. You are going to get a full written report every 10,000 miles so that you can make decisions and make plans to have the car serviced and cared for, even if it's over a period of time in the future. That's how we approach your lifetime maintenance!

The last thing you want to say is, "Hey, I'm just going to go buy another car." If you had a $10,000 car— and only 6% of the money is being spent per year on the care of that vehicle at eight years—somewhere in the neighborhood of $600 is what it will cost you to have it cared for in maintenance and repairs. A lot of times people will see a large repair cost and say, "Well, that's more than the car is worth." That's not always the case. On average right now, according to a report by *Experian* (published in the 4th quarter of 2012), most used cars are financed at **130% of their value**. Realizing that you'll lose a large amount of the value of your vehicle in the first few months due to depreciation, many times it still makes sense to keep an older vehicle and maintain it. Even if a few parts do break, it is better to repair it than to replace the car.

In the **Parkway Lifetime VIP Program**, we change the oil, the filter, and do the labor every 5,000 miles at no cost to you. You buy the club membership, and that entitles you to the free service. It also entitles you to the tires being rotated at no cost, as well as two types of inspections. One of these inspections is $20 and the other one is absolutely free. So a lot of value is built-in to the VIP membership because we get to see your car on a regular, consistent basis. You're going to make sure that it's being well cared for, and you're going to minimize your expense by paying for the club membership up front, and your membership is fully transferable to your next vehicle.

As a VIP club member, you will also receive a used-car inspection at no cost as long as the car that you are looking at buying is replacing the car that's in the club. It doesn't apply for reasons other than that. You also get a discount on the labor cost for repairs that you have done on your car. Currently, we have that discount set at 10%, and that is another great benefit for being a club member.

And all of our Lifetime VIP members (as well as every customer) can enjoy our Free, Round-Trip Courtesy Shuttle to get you where you are going and back again.

You'll also be enrolled in our ***Royalty Rewards*** program where you will earn points for every dollar you spend with us. These points convert to cash rewards that you can redeem on a later visit. It's all part of doing everything we can to provide exceptional customer service.

Motor Club Memberships

Q. Are motor club memberships worth it?

A. I think motor clubs are usually a great benefit for the consumer. They can also give great peace of mind for the consumer who travels a lot. Undoubtedly, their primary focus is the consumer. I am thinking of clubs like AAA Motor Club or Cross Country Motor Club, the two big wheels in the industry.

When you travel, you can feel extremely vulnerable in a part of the country where you don't know anyone. These clubs will help find a repair facility, a tow facility, a hotel, and other things of that nature that meet a certain standard. So, you can have some level of expectation about what type of service you are going to receive—"this is what I'm going to get when I go here." For Parkway Automotive, being AAA-approved is important. They make sure we have the insurance and the warranty to cover our customers, and they know that we'll stand behind our product. They certify that we will not overcharge a customer because they're traveling. The customer can also have some level of trust in what that facility might be doing for them or whatever service they may be providing. I think a good way to get that level of trust is through car clubs such as AAA or Cross Country.

Breakdowns

Q. *If I'm a Parkway customer but not a member of AAA and I have a breakdown on the road, what should I do?*

A. Simply call our office and we'll be there to help. At Parkway Automotive, one of our staff is always on-call and wearing a pager. Our customers can reach us 24-hours a day, seven days a week.

If you have a breakdown or need help,

call (501) 821-6111. We will assist you 24/7.

We have that number printed on each repair order. Our customers know our number and know how to get in touch with us after hours when there is an emergency. We have assisted customers who were many states away. When they have had a problem, we have been there to take care of them!

Introduction to Maintenance

We need to begin here with a definition of maintenance, because the term "maintenance" is thrown around all over the place—from the HVAC industry to auto repair to your VCRs or DVD players or television sets. They all have "maintenance." So let's just start by defining maintenance. It really means *care* or *up keep*. Let's first discuss fluids.

Engine Oil

(Some of the information on pages 60-64 concerning engine oil is duplicated here for your convenience)

There is one fluid that everyone knows should be maintained and that is engine oil. Here is what's happening and why you must change your oil. Almost everyone in the world knows to change their oil, but many people don't know why. Years ago, our fathers and grandfathers taught us to change the oil in a vehicle every 3,000 miles. They were right, because all the contaminants from unpaved roads got into their engines. The fuel that was pumped from the gas pumps was not filtered very well. It would go into the gasoline tank of your car and make its way into the engine. So the combination of unfiltered dirty air, as well as fuel coming in that was dirty, would make it to the inside of your engine. The job of the oil was to grab the dirt and suspend it so that whenever you changed the oil, the dirt would drain out with the oil. If you waited too long, the oil could not suspend and hold the dirt any longer. It would sink to the bottom of your engine. That usually happened because you waited too long between oil changes, driving more than 3,000 miles. By changing the oil regularly, you flushed the dirt and contaminants out of the engine, and everything was fine.

Now, let's fast forward to today. What we find now is that we still have the same exposure, both with gasoline and dirty air. No matter where we go, we're going to run into that. What has changed is that we have increased technology in air AND fuel filtering, and we have also sealed the engines tighter as a result of fuel injection. We have seen technology improvements in the ability of oil to suspend the dirt. When you bring all of these factors into the equation, you have a situation where the oil drain intervals can be much longer than they were in the past. Two reasons for this are:

1. There aren't as many contaminants getting into the engine as before,

and

2. The oil has a better ability to suspend or hold dirt, so when the oil is drained, all the dirt is going to drain out with the oil.

These are the reasons that we can do a 5,000-mile oil change intervals—which is pretty common these days— instead of 3,000-mile oil changes. There are some cars that can go much longer than that, and I've seen some of them, but I would still recommend 5,000-mile intervals mainly because there are other things on the car that need to be inspected and looked at by the technician. The tires should be rotated so that you get even wear and longer life out of them. There are other safety and maintenance items on the vehicle that need to be inspected on a regular basis. Currently, in 2013, 5,000 miles is where I land my plane on servicing your car.

Transmission Fluid

Let's take this principle: *The oil suspends the dirt and the dirt drains out with the oil at each oil change interval.* Now apply that principle and apply it to transmissions. Transmissions don't pull in air, but transmissions (and this is actually true with every component on your car and everywhere fluids are involved) do have metal-to-metal contact, or the potential for metal-to-metal contact. They are also exposed to heat. ALL of that will break down fluid over time. However, we fortunately do not have to service the transmission every 5,000 miles. Most experts in the industry, when it comes to those who are in the field working on vehicles — transmission builders and those who are ASE-certified in transmissions — have advised servicing the transmission every 30,000 miles. Typically, the manufacturer will have some recommendation on that as well. Some manufacturers have gone to a completely sealed unit and offer a lifetime fluid when they build the vehicle. That approach has not gained a lot of popularity at this time, but that could change in the future. It's important for you to know about this, and it's even more important that you take your vehicle to a repair service facility where they are continually educating their technicians on these matters. Cars change rapidly, and you certainly don't want an out-of-date technician working on your vehicle.

So the transmission needs serviced about every 30,000 miles, especially if you're towing trailers of any kind (boat, utility, RV, etc.). If you're not towing and you don't do a lot of driving, then you could probably go as long as 50,000 miles. Regardless of the interval, most vehicles today will at some point in time need the transmission fluid removed and new fluid put in.

Differential Fluid

We can also apply that same principle to what is called the differential. On most front-wheel-drive vehicles the differential is a part of the transmission, while all rear-wheel-drive vehicles, the differential is a separate part of the transmission, but it too should be serviced. You can follow the same interval for it that you do the transmission. In a four-wheel-drive vehicle, there would be two of those differentials as well as a transfer case. In a two-wheel-drive vehicle there is just one differential.

Power Steering

These same principles and guidelines can also be applied to the power steering system. This system is predominantly a "closed" or "sealed" system, but over time this fluid needs to be changed to protect the components from wearing out from the inside. Remember that it is always less expensive to change the fluid that protects the part than to replace the part itself.

Brake Fluid

Unlike the previous aspects of maintenance, with brake fluid and coolant there is a measurement that can be made on these fluids to determine if it is actually time for them to be changed. Whenever a measurement is available, that is what you should use. The measurement for brake fluid being flushed out is 200 copper parts per million. Once it reaches that level, the fluid needs to be replaced.

Here's actually what has happened at that point and why this measurement is important. Brake fluid is *hydroscopic*, which means that if you left the can open overnight, the contents would be ruined. It would expire because it would absorb enough moisture to make it unusable inside your vehicle. It is **imperative** that you always keep the brake fluid cap tightly sealed.

Inside the brake system, the brake fluid is designed to absorb moisture because moisture deteriorates all the metal components that the brake fluid comes in contact with. Brake fluid is a hydraulic fluid that causes the brakes to be applied so the car will stop properly. But if you have ever boiled brake fluid—which hopefully you haven't—then you would know that when brake fluid boils it creates air in your system. If you've ever had air in your system, you know that your brake pedal goes to the floor and doesn't stop the car. So, when we talk about copper parts per million in the brake fluid, anything higher than 200 copper parts per million is the indicator that the brake fluid should be removed from the car and new fluid put in. Once it reaches 200 copper parts per million, it's reducing the boiling point of the brake fluid and that could potentially cause you problems. These problems would not be seen or felt during breaking, but more importantly, over time you will see the deterioration of brake parts, which can be very expensive.

Since we have started doing brake flushes on vehicles, we seldom have to replace brake calipers. A lot of the chain stores will want to put new calipers on your car as part of a brake job, but they typically are not needed. We have reduced the number of brake calipers that we have put on vehicles over the years by a considerable amount. That is a really good example of how the fluids in your car are cheaper than the parts that they protect. Really, you are saving money long-term by maintaining your vehicle at regular intervals. Most brake flushes currently cost less than $100, usually in the $60 to $70 range. You have to do them every two to three, maybe four, years—depending on the fluid measurement and the environment. In contrast, brake calipers cost upwards of $500 or $600.

Cooling System

The cooling system's primary component is antifreeze/coolant. It helps keep the engine from freezing in the winter and helps keep it cool in the summer. Some manufacturers have attempted to come out with their own long-life antifreeze. GM tried with a product called "Dex-Cool", a five-year antifreeze, but it just didn't make it. It ended up causing a lot of problems in the vehicles' cooling systems.

As with brake fluid, there is a measurement that can be made to determine when your coolant needs to be replaced. It is a measurement of the pH level, which is an indicator of the acidic protection that the fluid is capable of providing, and the freeze point. A pH level of 7.0 is neutral and indicates that the coolant is no longer protecting the soft metals inside your engine. It's like having straight water in your cooling system. So, we can have a reading that might indicate good protection of -20 or so, but a pH level that is too low or too high is not protecting the soft metals. Once these pH properties break down, the fluid no longer protects or lubricates parts like your water pump, nor does it keep the cooling system healthy. This combination isn't good because it can deteriorate the metal inside your cooling system, which shortens the life of your heater core, radiator, and cylinder heads.

As a side note, antifreeze/coolant is typically mixed at a 1 to 1 ratio. When we mix antifreeze with water, a synergy takes place whereby the coolant protection level goes into the negative degrees — negative 10, negative 15, negative 20 degrees of protection.

The cooling system should be measured at 10,000-mile intervals. Usually a cooling system repair will cost $500 to $1,000. In contrast, having the coolant flushed costs less than $100. You are saving long-term dollars by maintaining your vehicle on a regular basis.

We can look at the full spectrum of maintenance on a vehicle and know for a fact that <u>fewer mistakes occur when maintenance is regularly performed</u> than when a repair is done. When a technician is not taking bolts off and putting bolts back on, the chance of a mistake occurring decreases dramatically. There's also less down time for you as the customer. Most facilities keep the fluids necessary to maintain your car properly in stock at all times. Parts that are broken have to be ordered; they may be right down the street—or they could be a day or two away. Think about how long you might be without your vehicle for maintenance versus a breakdown due to lack of maintenance. It becomes very costly when we you don't maintain your car.

Air Conditioning

In Arkansas we have very hot summers. Few things are more frustrating than having your air conditioning blow hot air when it is over 100° outside.

Your air conditioning system is a sealed system. If you are low on refrigerant, then that means you have a leak somewhere. Having the air conditioning evacuated and recharged about every three to five years is a good maintenance guideline.

Here's how you're A/C system functions: The oil used to lubricate the expensive air conditioning components is actually carried by the air conditioning refrigerant. Over time, there is usually a small amount of refrigerant that is leaked out, and with that will be some oil loss. When you lose oil from your A/C system it's like losing oil from your engine. Most people know that if you run your engine out of oil, you'll damage the engine; likewise, when you lose oil from your A/C system you can do damage to your A/C "engine" (also known as the compressor).

The inside of some compressors looks like a very small engine. It has some of the very same components as your engine. It has pistons and rings and rods and a crank shaft—all the things that make your engine run are on a much smaller scale inside the A/C compressor, and so keeping that compressor lubricated is crucial to its longevity.

The air conditioning system is not something that you are necessarily going to see a regular maintenance interval for in your handbook, or even from a lot of professionals. But I'll tell you, in my professional opinion, having the system simply evacuated and recharged to the proper amount puts fresh oil in the system, allows better lubricity (ability to lubricate) to take place for the compressor, and will make the compressor last longer. Unfortunately, there is not a dipstick to check your refrigerant oil level like there is in your car engine. And due to the high pressures in the A/C system and the very

> *NEVER* attempt to recharge your air conditioning system by yourself!

low amount of refrigerant that should be used...

You should ALWAYS have your a/c system serviced by an ASE Certified Technician. It's just too dangerous to do yourself.

Keeping your air conditioning system serviced every couple of years is a great way to save money and stay cool in the heat of summer.

Testing and Diagnosis

Years ago a technician would spend five minutes diagnosing a car and five hours making the repair. For example, he would raise the hood, see that the water pump or intake manifold was leaking, then decide it was time to go to work. Today, however, we might spend five hours running tests and diagnosing the vehicle and five minutes repairing or putting a component on the vehicle. The cost of electronics is really what's driving this.

There are a lot more electronics on vehicles today. It is not unusual—if we look at a Cadillac Escalade or some of the hybrid cars or German vehicles, or even something as simple as a Ford Taurus—to find somewhere between five and fifteen computers on the car. Within that system of computers, they must all communicate with each other, and there's usually a main computer. That is called the Power Train Control Module, and all the other computers must communicate with that computer through what's called a CAN—Controlled Area Network. That is where all the other computers are communicating with this primary computer, and so as that takes place, the technician is tasked with the responsibility of not just reading a code (because any of us can buy equipment to read a code), but also for understanding all of the possible causes for that code and making an accurate diagnosis. It can become extremely complex very quickly.

An example for a very common code would be P301.

A P301 means that the vehicle engine cylinder number 1 has a misfire. You can find people at parts stores that can read that code and say, "Oh, you have a P301."— but that doesn't tell you what component you need to repair that misfire. A misfire—and this would apply to any cylinder—can be caused by compression, a spark plug, a spark plug wire, an ignition coil, or an intake manifold gasket leaking. You have all of these possible areas, and I have yet to mention a fuel injector or an injector driver inside the computer—anything that has to do with getting fuel in and air management to that cylinder. Fuel, air or electricity—a failure in any of those areas is enough to cause a misfire. Because there is not a single component that would replace and repair a P301 on every vehicle, what you need is a skilled technician who can take that P301 and begin the process of testing to determine what component has actually failed. He can then give you an estimate to replace the component and repair the problem.

Car Care 301 *(or How To!)*

No book like this would be complete without a "How To" section. There are many things on a car that you can do yourself, and in this section I want to explain the proper way to do these.

How to Change A Flat Tire

Most vehicles today have a tire pressure monitoring system that will indicate that you have a low tire. Technology has increased to the point that it will actually tell you which tire is low, so be sure to pay attention to your dash lights. If that light comes on, you need to get to a safe place pretty quickly and see which tire is low. Tires will typically lose air and then go flat and they can do that over a short *or* a long period of time—depending on the size of the hole. *Pay attention to that.*

When you are in a situation where you need to change a tire, <u>the most dangerous place in the world for</u>

you to change it is on the edge of the interstate. If at all possible, get off of the interstate, even if that means driving on the shoulder at a very slow speed until you can exit—or at least to an area of the road where you are safely off the road. "Safely off the road" to me is at least 15 to 20 feet from the edge of the freeway where people are driving 65 to 70 mph. Ideally, you would be able to take an exit and get completely out of sight of the freeway to a safe location where you can raise the car up using the tools provided. A lighted area is preferable if this happens at night.

What I have done with each of my children is allow them to change a tire on their car at home in the garage, on a level surface so that I could at least show them the techniques. They should know how to use the tools. The best way to do that is to simply get your owner's manual out. Look what it says about changing a tire, be familiar with where the tools are, and actually go through the process.

The owner's manual will tell you the exact location that you must place the jack in order to raise the vehicle up safely. You can cause damage to the car or get injured if you place it in the wrong place. It's also best if, using their tools, you loosen the lug nuts that hold the wheel in place before you jack up the car. Do not take them off! Just break them loose. Give them about one turn to the left to break each one loose, then go ahead and jack up the car. That way, they are all loose and you can take them all off easily.

When you're going to put the tire(s) back on, be sure to start each of the lug nuts by hand. Turn them to the right and start each one, then run them down as far as you can with each hand. After that, you should tighten them in a star pattern. To do this you would tighten one then skip one, tighten one then skip one. This will eventually have you tightening all five lug nuts until they are all tight. Be sure to pay attention and <u>put the beveled edge of the lug nut toward the wheel</u>.

A lot of the cars come with the wrench that you would use to tighten the lug nut. One thing you can do to make changing the tire easier is to position the wrench in such a way that you can stand on it and use your leg and body weight to loosen each lug nut. However, you do not want to do that while tightening the lug nuts (because you can over-tighten them). Tighten all of the lug nuts, then after driving 50 to 100 miles, check them again and make sure they are still tight.

The best recommendations I can give?

1. *Practice changing a tire on the car you drive,*

2. *in your driveway,*

3. *on a flat surface,*

4. *where you're familiar with everything.*

5. *You <u>do not</u> want to change a tire for the first time on the side of a busy highway!*

How to Jump Start a Car

When we jump start a car, what we are trying to do is control a spark. The reason you want to control a spark is that one of the batteries might be venting acid gas—either the battery that has failed or the battery that you're using to jump the car.

What we mean by "venting" is that the battery fumes from the acid inside the battery are slowly leaking out of the top of the battery. That is a fairly common thing to see. Acid is explosive, so if you cause a spark, you could potentially blow up the battery. You would most likely have your face over it when that happens, and that could cause a different type of problem, to say the least. If you have safety glasses, it would be a very good idea to wear them. Safety glasses are about $1.50 at most places. I have a pair of these in my vehicle so that if I need to jump start a car, I would definitely put them on to protect my eyes.

Here's how to properly jump start a car:

First we connect the jumper cable to the ground (negative terminal) of the "good" battery. Next, connect the other end of that cable to the ground (negative terminal) of the "bad" battery.

Then connect the other cable to the positive terminal of the "bad" battery, and finally connect the final cable to the positive terminal of the "good" battery.

You're basically making an electrical circuit because the battery that is "hot" (the good one) is producing the electricity that is going to come from the positive side of the good battery. Making the last connection to the positive terminal of your good battery will minimize the possibility of spark, thus keeping you safe.

<u>How to Jump Start a Car</u>

| Good Battery   "Dead/Bad" Battery

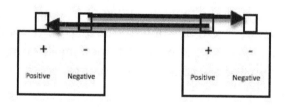

Connect Negative Good to Negative Bad,

THEN

Connect Positive Bad to Positive Good.

When Jump Starting a Car, Just Remember:

Good, Bad, Bad, Good

1) Negative Good —> 2) Negative Bad

3) Positive Bad —> 4) Positive Good

To remove the jumper cables, simply <u>reverse</u> the order.

How to Manage A Breakdown

You should be familiar with your gauges and know what "normal" is so that when the gauges are not within normal range, you will know that something is wrong. If you never look at the gauges, you won't recognize a normal reading. (*See **Gauges** section of this book, pg. 46*)

If you are driving and begin to feel something in the function of your car that you are unsure about, cautiously begin to move over into the right lane. *You do not want your vehicle to be disabled in the left lane or in the median of a freeway.*

Always try to get to a safe location to manage a breakdown, not only for the sake of your passengers and yourself, but for your vehicle too!

If your vehicle is beginning to overheat, certainly keep an eye on the gauges. They will indicate any overheating. If your vehicle *is* overheating, turn the engine off as soon as possible. You don't want to wait for more symptoms.

The second thing you should do during a breakdown process is to make a call. These days most people carry cell phones. Unfortunately, most people do not have a towing service, a motor club they could call, or a working relationship with a repair shop that has after-hours contact. If you find yourself needing help, you can always call our **Parkway Automotive office at (501) 821-6111**. We'll be happy to assist you.

Make sure that you're in a safe spot and that any passengers are a safe distance from the highway. You don't need anyone walking around the car with the risk of an accident occurring.

Managing a breakdown is really pretty simple, though many times nerve-racking. Always try to remember the following:

1. Don't panic!

2. Think "safety."

3. Call for assistance.

If you find yourself needing help, call our office 24/7 at (501) 821-6111. We'll be happy to assist you.

How to Manage An Accident

Because you would naturally be nervous managing a car accident, it will be in everyone's best interest if you practice. You will naturally be frightened and, depending on the severity of the accident, you could be crying and emotional. Even something as small as a minor fender-bender or a slow-speed parking lot accident can be enough to create emotion.

When you are in an accident, the first thing you need to realize is that insurance companies are the ones who typically determine who is at fault—so you don't want to readily admit that you are at fault. First, you should have your insurance information in the glove compartment to give the other party. Second, you want to get proof of insurance from the other driver. You need to make a call to the other driver's insurance company as soon as possible. If they have the necessary information available at the scene, call immediately to verify that they do have coverage. Just because the paper says they are covered doesn't mean they are. If they have let their premiums lapse, then they will not have coverage and you need that information as soon as possible. You certainly want to call the police as well.

You should also know that in the state of Arkansas—and this is true in most states—if there's no bodily injury, you are to remove the vehicle from the road. You can get a ticket for obstruction of traffic if you keep your car on the road and there's no personal injury. Remove your car to a safe place and proceed to work out the details with the other party.

A great reason to have a relationship with a repair facility is that if your car is not drivable as a result of the accident, you want to have it towed to the repair facility, even if they don't do body work! The repair facility is a safe place to store the vehicle until the other details of the accident can be worked out with the insurance companies.

The tow trucks that are dispatched by the police are under contract with the police. They will tow your vehicle to their impound lot and charge you a considerable amount of money to keep it there. In fact, that's how most tow companies make their money—through storage from accidents. **They make more money from storage of your vehicle than from the act of towing it.** A good reason to have a relationship with a repair facility that you can reach during and after hours is so that you can have them dispatch a tow truck to your location and have your vehicle towed back to their lot. **Most repair facilities will allow the car to remain there, free of charge, while the insurance company details are completed. This will save you hundreds of dollars in storage fees.**

If you have an accident, you can choose your own tow company. If the towing company that comes to the scene is under contract with the police department, then they will try to tell you that they have to take your car to their lot. **Do not allow them to do that.** You, as the owner of the car, can direct them to tow your car to your home or a repair facility of your choice; **but do not allow them take it to their lot because that will cost you a lot more money.**

Anyone reading this may call Parkway 24/7 at 501-821-6111 and store your car with us at NO CHARGE.

How to Manage Being Stuck in Traffic

There is one thing that I have learned to do, one thing that has even become a habit—and I can even give you a story of how I avoided an accident simply because of this habit! The habit is this:

When I am coming up behind a vehicle, about to come to a complete stop, I will stop far enough back from the car in front so that I can see the back tires of that car touching the ground. If I'm back that far, then I have enough room to maneuver around that vehicle if I need to for whatever reason.

The story I promised you: I was on my way home and had just topped a hill. Some construction workers had traffic stopped and, as is my habit, I stopped so that I could see the tires of the car in front of me touching the ground. The construction workers had the traffic on our side of the road stopped, and had just finished clearing the traffic in the left-hand side of the road and were about to let us go past. Suddenly, I heard brakes squealing, and in my rearview mirror I saw a car coming at me at a high rate of speed with all four wheels locked. Because I knew that I had stopped soon enough in front of the other car—back far enough to see their tires—I turned to the left and accelerated, quickly putting myself in the left lane where there was no other traffic. The car that had been coming at me skidded to a stop about two feet from the car that had been in front of me.

My habit of stopping far enough back saved me from being hit from behind. If the car had hit me, it obviously would have forced me into the other car that was in front of me. Everyone moved along, and when we got to a stop sign down the road, the lady in the car that was in front of me got out, came back to me and said, "Thank you. You probably saved my children from injury."

She had seen it all happening and could do nothing, but I was able to move my car out of the way. It was just one of those quick responses that was possible without thinking because I had made stopping a car-distance back a habit. You could even apply this in a carjacking. If someone were to decide to carjack you, you could easily accelerate around the car in front of you. Regardless of the situation, this is a good habit to develop.

That is my first recommendation for managing traffic. Just having a way out can be extremely helpful and beneficial.

Sometimes traffic jams simply cannot be avoided. Certainly, it would be good to <u>always keep more than a quarter tank of gas in your car</u>. You never know when you're going to get stuck in traffic.

Always watch your temperature gauge. Most cars are designed to be able to stand in traffic for a long period of time with the air conditioning on, but you should definitely keep an eye on your temperature gauge. You may have to roll your windows down and turn your air conditioner off so that the car engine doesn't get too hot.

Another aspect to consider is that traffic jams also occur during winter. In the northern parts of the United States, the law requires that you have a safety kit inside your vehicle. Usually, it contains some water, a blanket, a flashlight, and some other indicators to let other drivers see that you have broken down. And even in southern states like Arkansas, it's a good idea to carry a safety kit with you because you never know when you'll be stuck in traffic.

How to Drive on Snow and Ice

Snow and ice certainly provide different challenges for us who live in the southern states. When you are driving on snow you need to have more traction. That's why you'll typically see four-wheel-drive vehicles or front-wheel-drive vehicles getting around better—simply because their traction is much better. That does not mean that you should drive faster. It just means that you have better traction and should be able to get around a bit better.

When there is a lot of snow, one tip you can follow is to **lower the air pressure in your tires** to about 25 pounds of pressure. You are not going to be going very fast, but you are going to see that you'll have better traction when your tires have less pressure in them since you have more rubber on the road.

We learned years ago to pump the brakes in the snow, but the best advice I can give for driving in snow is to drive as though you had an egg under the gas and brake pedals. Drive so that you are accelerating slowly and braking slowly. Don't push on the pedals too strongly. You'll break the eggs!

How to Buy a Used Car

Say you've decided that you are going to replace your car. Or maybe you're buying a car for the first time and you want to begin with a used vehicle. You make the decision to buy a Ford F-150, four-wheel-drive truck. You are going to spend some time looking around. You might shop online and see some of the options available for a Ford F-150. There are four-door trucks, some with extra cab space, others with short beds and some with long beds. There are many options available, so you begin to narrow your search to match your criteria deciding, "I want a Ford four-wheel-drive, F-150 Lariat because it has the leather, and I want the four doors, and I want a CD player, and I want the five-and-a-half-foot bed, not the six-foot bed."

Once you've narrowed your search, it's time to actually begin looking for those that may be for sale. You can look on Craigslist. You can look on eBay. You can look in the newspaper or drive around town shopping. After looking around, you will find your vehicle. You are going to go view it, walk around it, look at it from a cosmetic standpoint, sit in it, and touch everything that you can touch. You're going to make sure everything works. The turn signals, the radio, the air conditioner, the heater, the power windows, the power locks, the power seats, the rear wipers, the front wipers, the headlights, the tail lights, and on and on.

If everything checks out, you tell the person who's selling the truck, "Look, I'm going to go spend about 45 minutes to an hour driving this." Most people spend about 10 minutes, and they go, "Oh, I like it." One of the reasons that you like it is because it's different from the vehicle that you just got out of, and all your senses are going, "Oh, this is really neat," and so you think, "Oh, this is the truck!" Give yourself 45 minutes to an hour. During this time you're going to be listening to and feeling things about that truck—and you don't have to be an automotive mechanic to know if something is not right. You'll know if a noise that you heard is not right or if there's something that doesn't feel right in the steering or a vibration in the brakes. And so, that 45 minutes to an hour should be spent driving both on the freeway at highway speeds and in town at normal speeds. You should spend time driving around, going around corners, stopping, accelerating—just as you would drive the vehicle normally on any given day. Use your senses. Don't play the radio. Make sure the radio plays, but after that turn it off and listen. Use your five senses to see if anything seems abnormal.

If everything seems good in this F-150 Lariat four-wheel-drive, everything sounds fine, and you really think you've found your truck, then take the truck to an ASE-certified technician for a used-car inspection. A used-car inspection is where a trained individual drives the truck around to check it out. Not only that, but also the technician will bring the truck back into the bay and raise it up. They're going to see things you can't see. They're going to look for things you can't know to look for, and they're going to know about things that you have no idea about.

Through this process, the ASE-certified technician can help you make a decision about repairs that may need to be done now or in the near future and can tell you the costs of those repairs.

Now you can say, "I love this truck. It's got everything I want. I've spent a lot of time looking and driving around and this is the one. So what will it cost to get these items up-to-date?"

Typically, the technician will provide an estimate for you. Then you can go back and negotiate your price for that vehicle. You should not talk about price, make an offer or say anything about price until you have taken all these steps.

Now, you're able to go back to the seller and say,

> "I've had it inspected. I've test-driven it. I want the vehicle. This is the one I want, but here is a list of things that are going to need fixed to make the truck the way that I want it to be. So, this is what I'm willing to pay for the truck so I can afford to get these other things done—and I will pay for it now."

THAT is the right way to buy a vehicle. Constrain your emotions, have a certified technician inspect it and know what you are getting into before you make an offer. By following this process you will save yourself from some unpleasant surprises that could cost you a lot of money.

How to Find a Good Repair Shop

If you are trying to locate a shop, the first thing to do is actually ask the shop that you're currently doing business with. I'm thinking of a scenario where you have moved out of town or to another state—first, ask the shop that you already know and trust if they can help you locate a shop in the area that you are moving to. Most of them have some type of associations that can help you locate one. So, that's a quick and easy way.

But let's say you've moved to another town and want to find a shop you can trust. What I recommend is that you schedule an appointment to go into that shop to have your car serviced—usually something simple like a tire rotation or an oil change. When you schedule your appointment, I recommend that you tell them that you're going to wait while that service is done. While that service is being performed, just listen to the interactions of the employees and other things that are going on. I know that you're not going to see everything, but that can tell you a lot about how they answer the phone, how they interact with the other employees, and how they interact with their vendors. Things of that nature that can help you answer the question, "Is this a professionally run shop or is this not quite the shop I want?" That can go a long way in helping you make your decision.

You certainly want to look at whether their technicians are certified. You want to figure out whether they do ongoing training, and determine to what extent they can service your particular car. Do they have the software to be able to communicate with the computer systems on your vehicle? You want a place that can send you reminders whenever it's time for service, a place that has some type of schedule to keep your car well maintained, a place that has an inspection process established where you can have your vehicle inspected for safety and maintenance items on a regular basis. That's an easy way of finding a good repair shop—just going into it, observing, and asking questions.

Five Questions to Ask Any Shop

If you are not able to go to the repair shop, but just want to call, then there are five simple questions that you can ask any shop as you make those

phone calls. I'll say this: <u>one of the most dangerous things that you can do is determine which repair shop you will go to based upon price</u>. Oftentimes, shops have strategies in place to give you part of the information or very little information about a particular repair, making their estimate "not quite accurate."

When it is time to pick up the phone and give some shops a call to answer the question "Which shop am I going to choose?", here are five questions you need to ask:

1. What is your warranty?

At Parkway Automotive, our current warranty is two years unlimited mileage on parts and labor.

2. Do you have a guarantee?

Most shops don't even think about a guarantee. At Parkway we offer a 100% risk-free, money-back guarantee—if we can't repair an item within three visits, we will give you 100% of your money back. That's our guarantee.

3. Are <u>all</u> of your technicians ASE-Certified?

Every technician at Parkway is ASE-Certified. Myself and two other team members are ASE Master Technicians. ASE Master Technicians are incredibly well-trained. So, no matter who works on your car at Parkway Automotive, they have ASE Certification in the area that they are working in. Even our service advisors are ASE-Certified! Basically, the question is this: "Can you guarantee me that whoever works on my car will be ASE-Certified?" And unless every single person in their facility is ASE-Certified, they cannot guarantee that.

4. Do you provide a free round-trip shuttle?

Parkway Automotive provides a free round-trip shuttle wherever you want to go in the Central Arkansas area. We know you need help whenever your car is down. A good repair shop should be able to provide a shuttle ride for you.

5. What happens if I have trouble when you're closed?

At Parkway Automotive, you can call us 24 hours a day, 7 days a week. You will be able to reach one of our people either by calling us directly during business hours or, after hours, you will receive an after-hours number to talk to an actual live human! Additionally, one bonus that we have is that you also earn rewards back on your repair as a Royalty Rewards member.

Those are five simple questions to ask any shop that works on your car. If the shop can answer all five questions satisfactorily, you have found a good repair shop.

How I Became "The Auto Guy" (*the rest of the story*)

In 1999 I started advertising on a local Christian radio station. One day, Jason Harper from a local television station, KATV Channel 7, heard one of my ads. He contacted me about doing a segment for Channel 7 on winterizing a car. I completed that segment and the producers liked what they saw, so they invited me back a couple of times. Soon after, they asked me to be on every week, and that was the birth of "The Auto Guy".

I was on Channel 7 for over ten years. Viewers would call in and ask questions about their car and I would answer them live on-air. It was a fun time for me and really kept me on my toes. I had to use everything I had learned up to that point to ensure I was giving these people the right information that they could trust.

This was a great experience for me that I may do again sometime. I think people liked the idea of having someone they could ask questions of and build a relationship with—even if it was through a TV show. People like to do business with people they know, like and trust. Becoming "The Auto Guy" has helped me to build those types of relationships with many in our community. Go to YouTube and search "The Auto Guy Parkway Automotive" and you will see my smiling face, or scan this QR code with your Smartphone.

Restoring the Corvette with John

It all started with my son John. He's my youngest of four children. When he was 12 years old, he came to me and said, "Dad, for my first car, I would like for you and me to build one." Of course, that went directly to my heartstrings, being "The Auto Guy".

So I said, "Sure, we can do that. What do you think you'd like to do? What particular kind of car?" And he said, "Well, I don't know. I'll look and let you know."

Some time went by, and he came back to me and said, "Dad, I think I want to build something in the '70s." I said, "Really? Well, that's good—because I can do those in my sleep and with my eyes closed and everything else. Do you have a particular one in mind?" He said, "I think I want a Corvette from the '70s." I said, "Okay, why don't you start looking?"

So he started looking at the cars, and he found some options on eBay. I made a promise to my wife that we would see, touch, and drive the car before we bought it. After some months had passed, in which he had been looking around, it was early one Saturday morning when I received a text message. John had spent the night with a friend, and I received a text message that the bidding was almost up on a car that was on his watch list. So I went upstairs, got on the computer, and looked at the car. It looked real good. I put a bid on it, and wouldn't you know... I won it!

Then, I sheepishly went back downstairs and climbed into bed beside my wife. She said, "What have you been doing up there?" I replied, "Uh, I found John a car, and I think I bought it. But I said I've only committed to it, and as I promised, we want to go look at it before we buy it. That's what I told the seller." She said, "That's good. Where is it?" I said, "Kentucky."

Later that day, I had to pick up John at his friend's house. As I was driving back home, I called the bank to see what time they closed. They told me the time they closed, and that's all I said. I hung up the phone, and John looked over at me and said, "You bought a Vette, didn't you, Dad?" I replied, "Well, no, I've committed to one—and it's in Kentucky. And we're leaving tonight to go look at it." So, on Saturday night at nine o'clock, my three boys and I got in the truck, hooked up the trailer, and drove as far as we could drive that night. After staying in a hotel room, we got up early the next morning, had breakfast together, and then finished our drive to this guy's house in northern Kentucky. It was a real nice road trip for us.

When we got there, we looked at the car, we drove the car, and we put the car up on the trailer and crawled underneath it to look for any signs of rust or deterioration. The car looked pretty good.

I pulled John aside and said, "John, it's going to be a lot of work. You've got to be committed, and you're going to pay for it. Are you sure this is what you want to do?" He said, "Yes, Dad, it's what I want to do." I said, "Okay."

So we bought the car, loaded her on the trailer, drove back home, and got home at ten o'clock that Sunday night with the car. Before we started disassembling the car (it was in really good condition, ran and drove well and was just a really good old car) we cleaned the car up externally for three days, and his sister used it in her wedding for her and her new husband to drive away in. This is before we did a single thing to it, so it was pretty cool.

After the wedding, we decided to begin the disassembly. Currently (Spring 2013), the car is in a thousand different pieces in our garage. But we are working to put it all back together with a new engine, new transmission, new wiring harness and a new interior. We are not going to do anything to the body because it is in really good shape—we are going to leave that alone. We are going to install air conditioning and get all that working. Hopefully, we will have it done by the end of 2013. John turns 16 in January of 2014, so he may very well be driving his Corvette then. That is what we are hoping for.

Father-Son Bonding

The most important thing in the world to me is the gospel of Jesus Christ. As John and I have worked on the Vette, there have been many extraordinarily easy parallels to make: we had an opportunity to talk about restoration because we were restoring a car! Of course, a car is not nearly as impactful or important as our relationship to the Lord and being restored through regeneration.

John has made it clear in the past that he wasn't sure about the gospel. He was pretty sure he didn't believe what we believed, and it was a good conversation. Recently, he has had a paradigm shift in his mind and heart. He has been studying God's Word, reading in Colossians on his own, and doing some things that indicate to me that the Lord has been working in his heart.

That's the biggest thing about spending time with him—just getting to know him more. We are working together to clean and restore, and I'm praying that as we do that, the Lord is cleaning and restoring his heart and mine.

Final Thoughts

I'm one of the most blessed people I know. I am "living my dream" by running my own company and serving my customers. I am loved by a beautiful woman who stands by me through good times and bad, have four terrific children, and am still in good health.

Not everything in life is rosy, but I've learned to find the good in almost every situation. My attitude and work ethic came from Mom, "washing the truck" from Brent Tyrrell, and the joy of being "the boss" comes from my excellent Team members at Parkway Automotive.

All of this is possible because of the grace of my Lord and Savior Jesus Christ. All that I have and all that I am is due to Him. At the end of each day, I am grateful that I am His son.

I hope you will choose to entrust Parkway Automotive with your vehicle needs. I can promise you that we will do everything in our power to ensure your satisfaction and the safety of your family.

Thanks for reading this book. I hope it has been helpful and has given you a better perspective on who I am and Whose I am.

Yours gratefully,

Mike Davidson
"The Auto Guy"

About The Auto Guy

Mike Davidson opened Parkway Automotive in January 1997. He's an ASE Master Certified Technician and was the Napa ASE Technician of the Year in Arkansas 6 years in a row. He serves on the Board of Directors for the Arkansas Better Business Bureau and was recently featured on the cover of Ratchet and Wrench Magazine.

Mike and Nancy, his wife of 23 years, have four children. They attend The Bible Church of Little Rock and are passionate followers of Jesus Christ.

How to reach The Auto Guy: (501) 821-6111

www.ParkwayAutomotive.net www.miketheautoguy.com